The Pocket Essential

BILLY WILDER

First published in Great Britain 2001 by Pocket Essentials, 18 Coleswood Road,
Harpenden, Herts, AL5 1EQ

Distributed in the USA by Trafalgar Square Publishing, PO Box 257, Howe Hill
Road, North Pomfret, Vermont 05053

A CIP catalogue record for this book is available from the British Library.

ISBN 1-903047-36-6

9 8 7 6 5 4 3 2 1

Book typeset by Pdunk
Printed and bound by Cox & Wyman

To some friends who fostered my love of reading and writing, each one a Mensch: Donald K Anderson, Jr, Bill Blaker, Douglas Hunt, Patricia Swann, Peter Wolfe

Acknowledgements

I thank most of all Rebecca Berg for her expert editorial work. Her knowledge, thoroughness, and sensitivity to language have sharpened both the writing and the insights in this book. Her precision and promptness sped its completion. Series editor Paul Duncan made excellent suggestions in shaping the manuscript. I also thank Donna Burney, David Flanagin, Millard Kimery, Evelyn Romig, Denise Venable and Beth Willingham, who helpfully commented on portions of the manuscript, and Elizabeth Wallace and the Faculty Development Committee at Howard Payne University, who provided a grant.

CONTENTS

Billy Wilder: A Certain Amount Of Charm

Billy Wilder is telling a story, something he does very well. He's in a seminar at the American Film Institute, talking about how he works with actors. Shortly before shooting began on *The Apartment,* Wilder says, he and his writing partner I A L Diamond needed to replace one of the leads. The nature of the role made it desirable to cast someone who was likable but who would also be convincing when revealed to be a cad. "We looked at each other," Wilder explains, "and both said simultaneously: 'Fred Mac-Murray!' Same intonation. 'Fred MacMurray!'"

MacMurray wasn't so sure. 'I can't do it,' Wilder quotes MacMurray as saying. 'I can't play a man who's got an illicit love affair in the apartment of one of my employees with the elevator girl and at Christmas yet.' Mac-Murray wanted to protect a lucrative contract he had with Walt Disney for a series of family films in which he would play, as Wilder tells it, "that *meshuggene* professor with the Volkswagen." MacMurray voiced his objections ("They would never forgive me! I'm through! I'm finished!"), and then Wilder attempted to change MacMurray's mind: "That took twenty minutes. Everything is possible if you've just got a certain amount of charm."

Charm is a useful byword for the career of Billy Wilder. His films often explore the charm of innocence and the charm of corruption, or to put it more precisely, the charm of corruption for the innocent and the charm of innocence for the corrupt. The director does not regard cloistered virtue as being very photogenic, but tainted virtue is another thing entirely. In his most serious dramas, characters who have compromised and corrupted themselves in tragic ways—like Joe Gillis in *Sunset Boulevard* and Chuck Tatum in *Ace In The Hole*—undertake too late to reclaim their integrity. In his comedies, characters whose desires are represented by the corruptions of worldly compromise and easy comfort—like Bud Baxter in *The Apartment*, Harry Hinkle in *The Fortune Cookie,* John Pringle in *A Foreign Affair*—relinquish their spoils and return gladly, if a bit stained, to the integrity they previously had no use for. Virtue becomes its own, more appreciated reward and vice its own punishment. Since the 1930s, Wilder's cinematic charm has been making audiences accept some unconventional truths and root for some unlikely heroes.

Perhaps Fred MacMurray also sensed that Wilder is one of Hollywood's anti-Disneys. A Wilder project, redeemed though it was by the charm of its writing and direction, nonetheless often addressed a subject in a way that offended the keepers of the status quo. This, of course, may simply be

another way of saying that Wilder puts his directorial charms and explora-
tion of innocence and corruption to the service of a realist's vision while
Disney prefers the eye of fantasy. The realist is usually the one whose work
elicits the sharp intake of breath from the audience when they sense that
things may not be the way they appear on the surface. As Wilder's character Barry Detweiler, a Hollywood producer, says in *Fedora:* "Sugar and
spice, and underneath that—cement and stainless steel." It's a bracing rec-
ipe, one that usually allows Wilder to adhere to his cardinal rule of film-
making: "Don't bore people, which is a very, very difficult thing... If you
have anything worthwhile saying better be very sure it is wrapped in choc-
olate so they will swallow it."

If in some ways Billy Wilder is an anti-Disney, what would a trip be like
to Wilderland, that imaginative theme park based on the spirit of his films?
It would, at least superficially, be eclectic. Wilder made films in every
genre of his day except the western. He made the pioneering film noir in
1944, *Double Indemnity*, which also starred Fred MacMurray (playing a
killer, the role that first made him fret about the safety of his career). What
came to be the staples of that genre—hard-bitten voice-over narration, a
dangerous femme fatale, urban landscapes shrouded in darkness both pho-
tographically and morally—are all on display in this landmark movie.
Wilder made the first film that took a realistic look at alcoholism (*The Lost
Weekend*), one of the first POW films (*Stalag 17*), and a handful of films in
various shades of light and dark that might be labeled 'fairy tales for
adults.'

Beyond these differences in genre, Wilder's films are unified by a fascination with the comic and dramatic possibilities of disguise and deception.
These disguises may be physical or psychological, intentional or uninten-
tional. In an often-reprinted essay that first appeared in *Film Comment*,
Stephen Farber points out that in Wilder's films relationships initially
made for convenience can unexpectedly produce genuine affection, just as
the shrewdness and wit required to swindle or exploit can win the director's approval. Farber states an important irony when he writes that 'deception is, in some twisted way, the one truthful, respectable act in the Wilder
universe.'

Contrarian

Wilderland may also be characterized as much by what is absent as by
what turns up. There is no self-pity, no sentimentalizing, no triteness, nothing saccharine. Wilder's brand of realism groups him with a particular type
of author. It is not the stylistic realism of slice of life but rather a realism

8

that questions assumptions. Imagine that throughout literary history there had been a society of like-minded writers named the Iconoclastic Authors League. Billy Wilder would be a member in good standing in this club of idol smashers—and not just because the group's initials match those of his long-time writing partner, I A L Diamond.

What names would appear on the roster of this heretical club? The founder might well be Euripides, the classical Greek dramatist whose play *Medea* fought received notions of male superiority and male smugness. Other literary iconoclasts in this group would be Voltaire, Jonathan Swift, George Eliot (really Mary Ann Evans masking herself with a male pseudonym), Mark Twain, Henrik Ibsen (whose dying words were "on the contrary"), and Bernard Shaw. One of Shaw's most quotable observations could even serve as the group's catchphrase: "All great truths begin as blasphemies." The contentious phrasing is something that only a true iconoclast would devise. Few will notice that Shaw does not claim all blasphemies become great truths but rather that you cannot find a great truth that did not come into the world overturning conventions and making people angry.

More importantly, Shaw's remark discloses the moral credentials of the Iconoclastic Authors League. The irony of many of these writers, Wilder included, is that they do not challenge conventional thinking simply to ruffle Disneyesque feathers, however satisfying that may be. Scratch an iconoclast, and you will often find a particular type of moralist, someone who recognizes the difference between morality and moral superiority. Iconoclastic thinking knows that conformity stultifies. Real human growth and insights become possible only after one is freed from the trappings of social convention. These moralists in horns cherish the insights gleaned from the rejection of conformity partly because such truths are hardwon.

Mensch

In spite of his acerbic, crusty reputation, Wilder has often been described as a moralist or even a romantic at heart. Under their astringent surface, his films consistently reveal a life-affirming quality. An attentive look at his movies should document both Wilder the idol smasher and Wilder the moralist. One of the best expressions of his voice of conscience appears in *The Apartment*. Jack Lemmon plays Bud Baxter, an accountant at an insurance company who has been lending his apartment to various married executives as a place to take their girlfriends. Bud's next-door neighbor, Dr Dreyfuss, hears what goes on through the walls and mistakenly thinks that Bud is a party-loving Casanova. "Slow down, kid!" the

9

doctor cautions in an early scene as Bud carries out another basket of empty liquor bottles. Later, after one of the women attempts suicide in Bud's apartment, Dr Dreyfuss saves her life and delivers to Bud some sterner advice: "I'd like to kick your keester clear around the block... Why don't you grow up, Baxter? Be a *Mensch*. Do you know what that is?... A *Mensch*—a human being." Wilder biographer Ed Sikov comments wonderfully on the scene: '[Dreyfuss] is the film's benevolent paternal figure... the man to whom Wilder entrusts the film's only moral....Be a Mensch doesn't just mean *be a real person*. It means *be a good and decent person*.'

The benevolent paternal figure in *Double Indemnity* is Barton Keyes, the claims manager at another Wilder insurance company, the aptly named Pacific All-Risk. Keyes is at the mercy of a "little man" in the pit of his stomach who ties Keyes into knots every time a fraudulent claim appears. This combination conscience/burglar alarm has never let Keyes down. He even admits to having checked up on his own fiancée after his little man started giving him trouble: "And the stuff that came out. She'd been dyeing her hair ever since she was sixteen. And there was a manic-depressive in her family, on the mother's side. And she already had one husband, a professional pool player in Baltimore. And as for her brother..." Only amid the sleaze and corruption of *Double Indemnity* would a man with such impossibly high standards and such a lonely obsession with integrity win the sympathy of the audience. In almost all of his films, Wilder tailors this life-affirming force to match his unorthodox point of view. In the dramatic films, it often represents conscience, although never in a preachy way; in the comedies, it often helps to bring together the lovers, removing psychological or plot-related obstacles in their path. One of the pleasures of a Wilder movie is the way Keyes' "little man" reappears in transformed and satisfying ways.

Writer

Wilder has usually described himself as first a writer, then a director. From his youth to the present, his work as a writer has shaped his view of the world. He was born Samuel Wilder in 1906 in the village of Sucha, south of Kraków, part of the Austro-Hungarian empire. His mother as a teenager had spent a long visit with an uncle in New York, and she fondly recalled cigar-store Indians and Buffalo Bill's wild west show. She nicknamed her son Billy and gave him a fascination for America. At some time between 1910 and 1916, the Wilder family moved to Vienna about 200 miles to the west. Wilder later left the University of Vienna where he was studying to be a lawyer and took a job at a newspaper. He worked as a crime reporter and pursued the Viennese elite for additional copy. He managed to interview Sigmund Freud, Alfred Adler, Richard Strauss, and Arthur Schnitzler. (Axel Madsen reports that all four interviews occurred on the same morning; Wilder has often said that Freud sent him away as soon as he learned that Wilder was a reporter.) Wilder's stories in 1926 about the concert tour of American musician Paul Whiteman led to Whiteman's offer for Wilder to accompany him and his band to Berlin.

After Whiteman and the band continued their tour, Wilder stayed in Berlin. He worked as a freelance reporter for various tabloids, magazines, and newspapers. His most famous series of articles described his activities as a gigolo at the Hotel Eden, or as he later explained it somewhat less luridly, as a tea-time dance partner for lonely old ladies. He also absorbed the disillusioned, decadent spirit and culture of the most notorious city in Europe. His artistic contemporaries were Bertolt Brecht, Kurt Weill, Thomas Mann, Fritz Lang, Erich Maria Remarque, Friedrich Hollander, and George Grosz. Wilder frequented the Romanisches Café on the Kurfürstendamm where such artists gathered. When later questioned about his artistic influences, he has usually mentioned the books of the American realists Mark Twain, Upton Sinclair, and Sinclair Lewis rather than the works of his Berlin contemporaries. Café society did suggest to Wilder, however, the potentially lucrative activity of ghost-writing in the German film industry.

The story of how he first sold a script may or may not be true, but it makes for a good anecdote: a naked producer clutching his trousers pounded on Wilder's door in a rooming house. The producer and his lover in another apartment had been interrupted by the unexpected arrival of her boyfriend. Giving the producer a place to hide, Wilder began pitching script ideas; soon, he had some cash for one of his screenplays, and the producer had his pants back. As it happened, the nervous gentleman was not a very high-ranking producer. Wilder later thanked the girl with the jealous boyfriend, but he also encouraged her to start up a flirtation with Erich Pommer, the production chief at UFA, the premier German studio.

One way or another, Wilder received his first screen credit in 1929 for writing *The Daredevil Reporter*, a chase film about kidnapped American heiresses and an intrepid newsman. His most noteworthy script from his years in Berlin was for *People On Sunday* (1929), which concerns the leisurely weekend outing of two ordinary Berlin couples who swim, picnic, and relax with others. Many of Wilder's collaborators on this film later distinguished themselves in Hollywood: Curt Siodmak and his brother Robert (whose idea the film develops), Fred Zinnemann (later the director of many classics, including *High Noon, From Here To Eternity*, and *A Man For All Seasons),* and Edgar G Ulmer (a director of lesser repute, mostly of mystery and horror films). Another important project was Wilder's script for *Emil And The Detectives* (1931), a story about a boy who mobilizes the youth of Berlin to help him apprehend a thief. Wilder received screen credits in Berlin for his writing work (mostly in collaboration) on thirteen films from 1929 to 1933. He not only eventually met Erich Pommer—and under perfectly respectable circumstances—but became, as Wilder's friend and fellow screenwriter Walter Reisch recalled, "Pommer's favorite writer."

When Hitler was named chancellor in early 1933, Wilder and other Jews in Berlin wondered what they should do. Wilder later told biographer Kevin Lally about seeing a team of SS men pounce on an old Jew and beat him to death, a brutality the Nazis called 'street theater.' The day after the Reichstag Fire, Wilder left Berlin on the night train to Paris. During the war his mother and other members of his family perished in the Holocaust.

In 1933 Wilder restarted his career in Paris. He was billed as the co-director (with Alexander Esway) and co-writer of *Mauvaise Graine (The Bad Seed),* about a teenage girl, played by Danielle Darrieux, who becomes involved with a gang of car thieves. Wilder's first directing experience was not a pleasant one. He was much happier when he successfully pitched an idea to Joe May, a former UFA producer, who was now working at Columbia Pictures in Hollywood. After nine months in Paris, Wilder had an offer of a steamship ticket to America and a weekly salary to develop his treatment into a script.

In Hollywood, Wilder learned English by conducting a very active social life and by listening to the radio, especially baseball games and Jack Benny. His first project at Columbia fell through, and after six months his visa expired. Stranded in Mexicali, Mexico, restricted by stringent immigration quotas, and hampered by a lack of documentation other than his birth certificate and passport, Wilder seems to have convinced an official at the US consulate to approve his return to America on the credentials of one sentence: "I write movies." The film-loving vice-consul stamped Wilder's passport and told him to "write some good ones." (Wilder, recounting the story at the 1988 Oscars, concluded: "I've tried ever since. I certainly didn't want to disappoint that dear man in Mexicali.")

Wilder eventually became a writer at Paramount, the studio with which he had his longest association. In 1937 he was teamed with Charles Brackett, an urbane, conservative New Englander and the opposite of brash, liberal Billy Wilder. But however clamorous their arguments (and Brackett is said to have thrown telephone books at Wilder in response to constant needling), the incompatibility resulted in some of the most brilliant scripts Hollywood has ever seen. Wilder terminated the partnership after *Sunset Boulevard*. He said that the creative spark was lacking with Brackett, but both men may simply have been worn down by their constant battles over taste. Wilder wanted to push the limits in developing their subject matter, and Brackett usually found such suggestions offensive. After working with a series of collaborators for one script each, Wilder has written his twelve most recent scripts with I A L Diamond.

Diamond had been born Itek Dommnici in Romania. His family moved to the US in 1929 when he was nine, and he grew up in Brooklyn. His father changed the family name to Diamond, and his son adopted the initials I A L when he started writing and needed a classy-sounding byline. He explained his choice by citing his consecutive championships as a schoolboy in the tri-state competition of the Interscholastic Algebra League. Most people, however, called him Iz.

A Wilder script has a tight structure and sharp, memorable dialogue. Often the final third of the script is still being written when shooting begins, a practice Wilder started in his early days in Hollywood to safeguard his continuing involvement with the project. Everything fits together in a Wilder script. Economy is important. He learned—maybe from Charles Brackett, maybe from Ernst Lubitsch, maybe through an intuition of his own—that the dramatic use of objects can reveal character, fuel the plot, develop an idea. Selected objects are often invested with emotional meaning in cinematically interesting ways.

Reading a Wilder script, one senses his true love of screenwriting. Even the descriptions of the sets show some flair. Bud Baxter's apartment, in the script published by the Praeger Film Library, is said to have 'lots of books, a record player, stacks of records, and a television set—21 inches and 24 payments.' Joe Gillis seems to speak for Wilder when he says in *Sunset Boulevard:* "Audiences don't know somebody sits down and writes a picture; they think the actors make it up as they go along." Another telling comment by Gillis appears to voice some of Wilder's frustrations with the writer's diminished lot in the assembly-line Hollywood system: "I wrote a script once about Okies in the Dust Bowl. You'd never know it because when it reached the screen the whole thing played on a torpedo boat." In a sense, Wilder's simple statement to the vice-consul in Mexicali was perhaps the most self-defining remark he could make: "I write movies." Louis Giannetti points out in *Masters Of The American Cinema* that Wilder is one of the few writers for the movies who is not a frustrated novelist, playwright, or poet. He is proud of being a screenwriter; he finally became a director, in fact, to protect the integrity of his scripts.

Director

Wilder's directorial approach reveals an austere elegance. Like many directors who started in the classical era of Hollywood, Wilder does not apply the elements of cinematic style ostentatiously. Craftsmanship comes through restraint. Insinuation and nuance are favored over flash and glitter. Axel Madsen, in one of the first books about Wilder, quoted the director's views on film style: "Helicopter shots, I don't mind—but not in the living room, please. There is a disregard for neatness in directing." It is not surprising that the sophisticated comedies of Ernst Lubitsch are one of Wilder's great inspirations, nor that for years Wilder has kept near his desk a sign that reads, 'How Would Lubitsch Do It?' These Wilder traits of directorial neatness and well-crafted scripts have left a legacy as impressive as that of any other film-maker. He has received 21 Academy Award nominations and six wins: one for producing, two for directing, three for writing. He is also a recipient of the Academy's Irving Thalberg Award. A director today could well ask, 'How would Wilder do it?'

For years, the type of visual restraint that Wilder favors in his films was dismissed as unimaginative. Today, however, when an ordinary soft-drink commercial features elaborate and expensive computer graphics, flash cutting, and special effects, the visual subtleties of a Wilder film seem like a refreshing change of pace. And for people who watch closely, the visual design bears out the comment of Stephen Farber that 'there is almost always a touch of flamboyance in the filmic details.' Wilder has often said that he admires elegant camerawork but nothing too fancy. In an interview with Chris Columbus in *American Film*, Wilder said: "There's never, never a phony shot in any of my pictures. Never one of those astonishing 'living room seen through the burning fireplace from the point of view of the roofer on top...' It's all logical, and you don't know where the cut is. I don't shoot it like a hack. I shoot it elegantly."

His accomplished directorial style and his sense of when cinematic points can be made visually rather than verbally are perhaps his most underrated talents. One of the most satisfying aspects of watching a Wilder film is appreciating the care put into the visual compositions. The effort devoted to achieving this transparent style is probably no less than that required for more eye-catching effects.

Collaborator

Over most of his career, Wilder was helped in this regard by some trusted, long-term collaborators. Doane Harrison worked on every Wilder film from *The Major And The Minor* in 1942 until Harrison's death in 1967. He began as an editor who received the great distinction of being allowed on the set during shooting. Later, his name appeared in the credits as editorial supervisor and, towards the end of his career, as associate producer. During filming, Harrison would advise Wilder when they had sufficient footage for effective cutting in the editing room. By not shooting extra establishing shots or close-ups to cover themselves, Wilder and Harrison eliminated the possibility that the studio could later recut the film differently. The individual shots were thus like the pieces of a jigsaw puzzle that could only be assembled in the one way the writer/director and editor wanted. (Wilder learned well from Harrison. When Ernest Walter, the first editor who worked with Wilder after Harrison's death, finished his work on *The Private Life Of Sherlock Holmes*, he said with admiration that little more was required in the editing than removing the clapper boards at the beginning of each shot.)

Shirley MacLaine, talking to Wilder biographer Kevin Lally, cited Harrison as Wilder's most unrecognized collaborator. She credited Harrison with the ability to elicit from Wilder some of his most compassionate moments on screen: "When Doane died, something went out of Billy. I began to realize what editors were in the lives of great directors. He'd say to Billy, 'You didn't break my heart today—go back and do it again.'"

Other great talents also worked with Wilder. Cinematographer John F Seitz was nominated for an Oscar for his work on each of the four Wilder films he photographed: *Five Graves To Cairo, Double Indemnity, The Lost Weekend,* and *Sunset Boulevard.* The most evocative and memorable musical scores in Wilder films have come from Miklós Rózsa, Franz Waxman, and André Prévin. The magnificent set designs of Alexander Trauner have appeared in many Wilder films since 1957.

The Wilder touch may be described, but of course there is still that element X, the intangible, the something that cannot be analyzed. As an example, consider a forgettable 1956 comedy called *Teenage Rebel*, directed by Edmund Goulding, about a girl whose prickly personality alienates her classmates. One after-school scene takes place at the counter of a malt shop. A boy tries to shatter the haughty girl's reserve by telling her jokes to get her to laugh. Suddenly, one realizes that this is the restaurant scene from *Ninotchka* retrofitted for teenagers. The jokes and dialogue are different, but the premise and the punch line of an adenoidal Melvin Douglas falling off his stool to raucous laughter are identical. Former Wilder and *Ninotchka* collaborators Charles Brackett and Walter Reisch wrote the script for *Teenage Rebel*, but that missing element X is all too obvious. Perhaps the best comment would be to adapt the words of Joe Gillis: "I wrote a script once about a woman from Russia and a Parisian falling in love in a French restaurant. You'd never know it because when it reached the screen the whole thing played in an American malt shop with juke-boxes and teenagers."

"I Write Movies"

The nature of the studio system makes it difficult sometimes to determine what writers worked on what projects. As he had done in Berlin, Wilder ghost-wrote at least two Hollywood films, *Under Pressure* in 1935 and the comedy *The Bishop's Wife* in 1947. Wilder also contributed the idea for the five-episode anthology film, *Tales Of Manhattan* (1942). He recycled the premise of a tailcoat being handed from person to person and the effect it has on their lives from an unproduced script he had written at UFA.

Music In The Air (1934)

Director: Joe May
Writers: Robert Liebman, Howard I Young & Billy Wilder, based on the operetta by Jerome Kern & Oscar Hammerstein II
Cast: Gloria Swanson (Frieda), John Boles (Bruno), 85 minutes

Ed Sikov reports that for his first screen credit Wilder was one of eight writers (credited and uncredited) who worked on this musical about a Bavarian teacher who writes a catchy tune and goes to Munich to try to sell it.

Lottery Lover (1935)

Director: William Thiele
Writers: Franz Schulz & Billy Wilder, from a story by Siegfried M Herzig
Cast: Lew Ayres (Frank Harrington), Peggy Fears (Gaby Aimée), 82 minutes

Wilder was one of a dozen writers working at various times to cook up this trifle about a sailor who wins a shipboard lottery for a date with a visiting Parisian dancer.

Champagne Waltz (1937)

Director: A Edward Sutherland
Writers: Frank Butler & Don Hartman, from a story by Billy Wilder & H S Kraft
Cast: Gladys Swarthout (Elsa Strauss); Fred MacMurray (Buzzy Bellew), 85 minutes

Wilder co-wrote a script about an American bandleader in Vienna and sold it to Paramount. The studio then assigned it to others for a rewrite. Wilder, however, landed his job as a contract writer at Paramount as a result of this sale.

Bluebeard's Eighth Wife (1938)

Director: Ernst Lubitsch
Writers: Charles Brackett & Billy Wilder, based on the play by Alfred Savoir
Cast: Claudette Colbert (Nicole de Loiselle), Gary Cooper (Michael Brandon), Edward Everett Horton (The Marquis de Loiselle), David Niven (Albert de Régnier), 84 minutes

Story: The romantic ups and downs of Michael Brandon, an American millionaire who has been married seven times, and Nicole de Loiselle, whose debt-ridden father encourages her to become wife number eight, play out against the backdrop of the French Riviera. Resentful of the way Michael weds, beds, and casts off wives, Nicole resists his advances after their wedding to quicken the inevitable and lucrative divorce settlement. Six celibate months later, a frustrated Michael agrees to the divorce. But the affectionate rancor of their marital squabbling has convinced Nicole that she really loves Michael. She pursues him to the sanitarium where he soothes his jangled nerves and finally gets him to admit the same.

The Verdict: Brackett and Wilder's first collaboration features some clever touches, but it really comes to life in only two scenes. One is the 'meet cute' suggested by Wilder that opens the film: Cooper, the miserly millionaire, is buying a pair of pajamas in a department store but refuses to pay full price since he only uses the tops; Colbert offers to pay the rest since she only wants the bottoms. Their flirtation thus begins in a way that foreshadows their eventual, if long delayed, consummation. The second effective scene occurs after their wedding, when Colbert chomps on an onion behind Michael's back before she agrees to kiss him. Her rank breath creates a recurrent joke throughout the entire scene. *2/5*

Midnight (1939)

Director: Mitchell Leisen
Writers: Charles Brackett & Billy Wilder, based on a story by Edwin Justus Mayer & Franz Schulz
Cast: Claudette Colbert (Eve Peabody), Don Ameche (Tibor Czerny), John Barrymore (Georges Flamarion), Francis Lederer (Jacques Picot), Mary Astor (Helen Flamarion), Elaine Barrie (Milliner), Monty Woolley (The Judge), 94 minutes

Story: Eve Peabody rolls into Paris on a rainy night asleep on a train. She has lost everything at the gaming tables of Monte Carlo except the evening gown she wears. She meets Tibor Czerny, a cab-driving philosopher who chauffeurs her from nightclub to nightclub in an unsuccessful attempt to get her a singing job. Tibor learns that Eve is a gold-digging chorus girl from Kokomo, Indiana. He himself is honest and poor and proud of it. He is also quickly falling in love with Eve, a realization that prompts her to run off into the rainy night. Using the name Baroness

Czerny to crash a high-society recital, Eve slips her pawn ticket from Monte Carlo to the doorman collecting invitations. She mingles with a group playing bridge, but Georges Flamarion, who has been watching her, suspects her masquerade. He secretly pays for her hotel room at the Ritz, sends her a trunk of clothes the next morning, and then arrives to explain.

Georges simply wants his wife back. He asks Eve to insinuate herself between Georges' wife, Helen, and her lover, Jacques Picot. As an inducement of riches to come, Georges tells Eve that Jacques draws a "very superior income from very inferior champagne." She accepts Georges' invitation to the Flamarion estate that weekend. Meanwhile, that mysterious pawn ticket for someone named Eve Peabody has made Helen suspicious that the 'Baroness Czerny' might really be the Kokomo chorine whose face she thinks she recognizes from a newspaper photograph. Georges overhears Helen's plan to expose Eve at midnight before the assembled guests, but he and Eve are philosophic: "Every Cinderella has her midnight." Suddenly, Tibor arrives, announced as the Baron Czerny, and the comedy of mistaken identities continues. Tibor has mobilized all the taxi drivers of Paris in a search for Eve. Now, this honest plebeian wants her badly enough to pretend to be a baron. Eve and Tibor engage in a comical contest of lies in their efforts to outwit each other. They finally wind up in a French court asking a judge to end their make-believe marriage. The judge refuses since Tibor is obviously insane.

Subtext: This lovely film, another of Wilder's cinematic fairy tales for adults, charts the romantic education of Eve Peabody, how she comes to understand that what she needs (Tibor and his integrity) is preferable to what she wants (Jacques and his money).

Background: The second teaming of Brackett and Wilder shows much more finesse than their previous script. Elaine Barrie, married to John Barrymore, appears in the small part of the milliner. The Richard Benjamin film *My Favorite Year* gives its Peter O'Toole character some of the legendary off-screen antics of Barrymore during the filming of *Midnight,* especially a bawdy trip to the ladies' room. Don Ameche never met Wilder until nearly fifty years later on the night of Wilder's tribute by the American Film Institute. In one of the highlights of the evening, Ameche humbly thanked Wilder for writing the part of Tibor Czerny, one of the best of Ameche's career.

The Script: Though the entire script is a jewel, the third act shines the brightest. The morning after Tibor's arrival at the Flamarion estate, he and Eve try to outsmart one another with their dueling fictions. Tibor invents an imaginary daughter with measles to get Eve to leave; Eve tops him with a fake phone call, after which she announces that their girl is fine. Before Tibor can appear in his working clothes and contradict Eve's lies, she anticipates him by telling the others that Tibor has spells of madness and that they must humor him. The more Tibor later insists on the truth, that he is nothing but a simple cabby, the more the house guests indulge the rantings of the eccentric baron. The nimble wit of Tibor and Eve recalls that of Kate and Petruchio in *The Taming Of The Shrew*, playing their own games of pretending that the sun is the moon and that an old man is really a young girl. For a truly enjoyable exchange of movie shop talk—one screenwriter savoring the classic work of another—read the comments by Cameron Crowe in appreciation of *Midnight* in his 1999 book *Conversations With Wilder*.

The Wilder Mensch: One of John Barrymore's best screen roles, Georges is Eve's "fairy godmother," a joke the trailer for the film repeats. By ostensibly indulging her worldly desires, Georges gets her to see, as he has, the satisfactions of real love.

Meaningful Objects: The pawn ticket Eve brings to Paris from Monte Carlo moves the plot forward and reveals character. It almost gets her ejected from the exclusive recital and tips off Georges to her impoverished state.

The Visual Element: Wilder always complained about director Mitchell Leisen (and vice versa), but this film seems to have deservedly escaped everyone's criticism. One nice directorial touch occurs with the delivery of Eve's large trunk—actually a wardrobe bought for her by Georges. The steamer trunk dominates the frame in the foreground as a bellboy opens and displays its rich contents while Eve in the background stares in wide-eyed uncertainty.

The Verdict: Not quite the brilliance of *Ninotchka*—but close. *4/5*

What A Life (1935)

Director: Jay Theodore Reed
Writers: Charles Brackett & Billy Wilder, based on the play by Clifford Goldsmith
Cast: Jackie Cooper (Henry Aldrich), Hedda Hopper (Mrs Aldrich), 75 minutes

Paramount wanted its own version of MGM's popular Andy Hardy series, and Brackett and Wilder were assigned to this first in a series of Henry Aldrich teen comedies. Henry must do well on his history test to get permission to attend the spring dance.

Ninotchka (1939)

Director: Ernst Lubitsch
Writers: Charles Brackett, Walter Reisch & Billy Wilder, from a story by Melchoir Lengyel
Cast: Greta Garbo (Ninotchka), Melvyn Douglas (Count Léon D'Algout), Ina Claire (Swana), Sig Ruman (Iranoff), Felix Bressart (Buljanoff), Alexander Granach (Kopalski), Bela Lugosi (Razinin), 110 minutes

Story: Three representatives of the Russian Board of Trade arrive wide-eyed in Paris. The job of Buljanoff, Iranoff, and Kopalski is to sell the jewels of the former Grand Duchess Swana, originally confiscated from the czar's family during the revolution. A Russian count working as a waiter alerts the Grand Duchess, who is also staying in Paris with her lover Léon D'Algout. Léon wines and dines the Russians, who are only too willing to compromise their Marxist ideals in capitalistic Paris. Léon initiates a lawsuit in an attempt to reclaim the jewels.

As a countermove, the Kremlin sends its special envoy, Ninotchka, to accomplish what the three Russians have botched. She meets Léon by chance on a traffic island, and he is attracted to her both before and after he learns of her involvement in the court case. Gradually, Léon and the charms of Paris—the Eiffel Tower, an outlandish but fashionable hat, the infectious laughter of a proletarian restaurant—crumble the façade of the stern Russian envoy. Now an eager visitor to nightclubs where she tastes her first champagne, Ninotchka becomes more heedless of the jewels, which are sneaked away by Swana's spy, the waiter. Possession of the jewels, however, drives home to Swana another truth—that she has lost Léon. The next morning Swana offers to relinquish the jewels if Ninotchka will return to Russia. "That's not the way to get him back," Ninotchka tells Swana. But Ninotchka goes anyway.

She's right. Denied a visa, Léon undertakes a one-man mission to get Ninotchka out of Russia. His letters are censored, and all his efforts seemingly fail. Later, Commissar Razinin must send Ninotchka once again to discipline Buljanoff, Iranoff, and Kopalski. During a night of carousing, they threw a carpet out of their hotel window in Turkey and then complained to the management that it didn't fly. When Ninotchka arrives in Constantinople, the three Russians tell her that they have defected and now own a Russian restaurant. She cannot imagine how they could have organized such a plan until her friends direct her to the balcony, where Léon awaits.

Subtext: A love story of opposites combines with a satire of officialdom. The film emphasizes love over ideology, humility over comic pride. The theme of regeneration—the word has an "ugly sound" to Swana—illustrates these changes. Léon becomes one of the first of Wilder's likable but soiled characters to reclaim his integrity. Beginning the film as Swana's little "Volga boatman" or kept man, Léon is ennobled by his love for Ninotchka.

Background: Greta Garbo, under contract to MGM, wanted to make a film with the great Ernst Lubitsch. Lubitsch eventually brought in Brackett, Wilder, and Walter Reisch to finish and polish the script. *Ninotchka* was the basis of the stage musical *Silk Stockings*, which was itself later a film with Fred Astaire and Cyd Charisse. A number of other actors were discussed for the Melvyn Douglas role, including Cary Grant, Gary Cooper, William Powell, and Robert Montgomery.

The Script: According to Scott Eyman, author of an excellent 1993 biography of Lubitsch, Brackett, Wilder, and Reisch wanted Lubitsch to receive a screen credit for his role in shaping the script. His work was primarily that of editor or "purifier," as Wilder called him. It was Lubitsch who overruled the earlier strategy of S N Behrman and Gottfried Reinhardt to have a nickel mine serve as the comic MacGuffin for the plot. Jewels were more photogenic, he rightly sensed.

The script brims with memorable moments, too many to itemize, but one easy-to-miss example helps to make the point. Much of the essence of good screenwriting appears in the brief exchange between Ninotchka and her girlfriend Anna, who plays in the orchestra of the Moscow Opera. Anna will soon be married, and Ninotchka gives the silk slip she wore back from Paris to Anna for her honeymoon. Heading to the opera for that evening's performance, the elated girl stops with the underwear in one hand and her cello in the other. "Am I going to play that cadenza tonight!" Anna says to Ninotchka. Those eight words confirm her eagerness for her honeymoon, her passion for music, her poverty in Moscow, and her gratitude to her friend. Revealing much with little—that is the poetry of good dramatic writing.

The Wilder Mensch: Buljanoff, Iranoff, and Kopalski were not comic characters in previous drafts of the script. Once Reisch, Brackett, and Wilder joined Lubitsch, they saw the full possibilities of these likable scoundrels. Their capitalistic corruption begins the film with a comic highlight. Their personal warmth also dispels some of the chill in the later Moscow scenes by giving Ninotchka confidants with a shared experience. These comrades and Ninotchka savor their Parisian memories, their closeness symbolized by the rationed eggs the four of them combine for their omelet. The three Russian buddies are the most life-affirming characters in the film.

Meaningful Objects: The writers were stumped over how to dramatize the change in the characters. Lubitsch came up with the idea of hats. Wilder learned well the lesson of how objects can reveal character, illustrate a theme, or advance the plot. A quick dissolve from the wintry headgear of Moscow to that of top hats and bowlers signals the ideological corruption of Buljanoff, Iranoff, and Kopalski. Later, Ninotchka secretly buys a silly hat she has earlier scorned. Once her inhibitions ease, she shyly models the new hat for Léon, a sign of her cautious love and changed outlook.

The Visual Element: Lubitsch often used doors in his films as a way of insinuating information slyly to the audience. As Wilder told writer David Freeman for a June 1993 *New Yorker* article, "Lubitsch can do more with a closed door than most directors can with an open fly."

The Verdict: Garbo's only comedy and perhaps her best performance, the film is a masterpiece of romantic comedy. *5/5*

Rhythm On The River (1940)

Director: Victor Schertzinger
Writers: Dwight Taylor, from a story by Billy Wilder & Jacques Théry
Cast: Bing Crosby (Bob Sommers), Mary Martin (Cherry Lane), Basil Rathbone (Oliver Courtney), Oscar Levant (Billy Starbuck), 92 minutes

This project began as the Wilder script *Ghost Music*, about two ghostwriters who really compose the hits of a famous songwriter. Like *Champagne Waltz*, this script was eventually handed to other writers.

Arise, My Love (1940)

Director: Mitchell Leisen
Writers: Charles Brackett & Billy Wilder, from an original story by John Szekely & Benjamin Glazer and a previous script by Jacques Théry & Ketti Frings
Cast: Claudette Colbert (Augusta Nash), Ray Milland (Tom Martin), Walter Abel (Phillips), George Zucco (Prison Governor), 110 minutes

Story: American soldier of fortune Tom Martin and foreign correspondent Gusto Nash meet and fall in love in Europe as war clouds gather. On 3 September 1939, they are traveling on the liner Athenia when it is sunk by the Nazis. They decide to put off their wedding and join the war effort.

Subtext: The film compares interestingly with Alfred Hitchcock's *Foreign Correspondent*, which also dramatizes the events of an American reporter caught in Europe in September 1939. Both movies are propaganda pieces that seek to deter American isolationism. Hitchcock's film emphasizes action and adventure; the Leisen-Brackett-Wilder movie is more romantic.

Background: The Claudette Colbert character is based on Martha Gellhorn, a correspondent for *Time-Life* and Ernest Hemingway's third wife. Colbert told the *Saturday Evening Post* in 1948 that Gusto Nash was her favorite among all her roles, a surprising admission since Colbert had appeared in many better-known movies. Ed Sikov speculates that the independence and intelligence of Gusto probably attracted Colbert to the character. The birthday (22 June 1906) on Tom's passport is the same as Billy Wilder's.

The Script: The project had passed through a number of hands before it reached Brackett and Wilder. The dialogue sounds like their work, but the three acts of the film's structure blend oddly. The first act is essentially an action-adventure story. Gusto, wanting first-hand information about a soldier of fortune, pretends to be Tom's wife to extricate him from a prison in fascist Spain. A car chase leads to an airplane chase before they make it safely to France. Act Two is a love story. In Paris, Tom tries to get Gusto to respond to him romantically, but she feigns indifference in order to concentrate on her career as a war correspondent. This act concludes when her editor Phillips assigns Gusto to Berlin. Act Three is a propaganda piece. The lovers interrupt Gusto's train trip to Berlin for a few days at an inn in the Forest of Compiègne. Now they are united in their love but torn over whether they should marry and plan a future or work separately for the cause of freedom, she in Berlin and he as a volunteer for the RAF.

The Wilder Mensch: Phillips, Gusto's harried editor, brings the couple together first by assigning her to do a story on Tom and then by helping Tom find her after her posting to Berlin. Walter Abel's likable performance injects some pleasing comedy into the film.

Meaningful Objects: A band aid on the nose indicates the fate of men who make unwelcome advances to Gusto. The morning after their escape from Spain, Tom sports a band aid; after his night in Gusto's hotel room, so does Phillips. When Gusto is still pretending to resist Tom, he gives her a typewriter ribbon as a going-away present, a playful symbol of her career-first approach to life. A luggage sticker for the American Line elicits a poignant reverie from a French maid who dreads another war and dreams of her sister's peaceful life in America.

The Visual Element: Mitchell Leisen uses close-ups effectively in the Spanish prison and in the Paris scenes; the studio back-projection of some of the outdoor scenes weakens the picture.

The Verdict: A curious movie that may be most interesting for what it reveals about its time. Perhaps the collective spirit of the coming war effort made audiences overlook the disjointed structure. *3/5*

Hold Back The Dawn (1941)

Director: Mitchell Leisen

Writers: Charles Brackett & Billy Wilder, based on a screen treatment and a novel by Ketti Frings

Cast: Charles Boyer (Georges Iscovescu), Olivia de Havilland (Emmy Brown), Paulette Goddard (Anita Dixon), Walter Abel (Hammock), Mitchell Leisen (Saxon), 115 minutes

Story: Georges Iscovescu, a Romanian gigolo, waits dejectedly in a Mexican border town for his quota number to enter the US. His dance partner, Anita Dixon, suggests he do what she did: marry an American and then get a divorce across the border. Georges thinks he has found his mark in Emmy Brown, a spinsterish schoolteacher visiting Mexico on a holiday. In one night Georges talks Emmy into marrying him; now, he must wait in Mexico four more weeks for his paperwork. After Emmy returns to her classes, he promises Anita that they can resume their act once he rids himself of his new wife.

Emmy, however, takes a week off and returns to Georges. To elude Hammock, a US official out to spot marriages made for immigration purposes, Georges suggests that he and Emmy honeymoon by car. During their week-long trip, Georges begins to regret his swinish behavior. Back at the hotel, Anita sees his change of heart and out of jealousy tells Emmy the truth about Georges' motives. Emmy's seven days with Georges have so touched the lonely schoolteacher, however, that she refuses to expose him to Hammock. Georges realizes that he loves Emmy, and he rushes to be at her side after she is injured in a car accident on her drive back to America. Recovered, Emmy returns to Georges.

Subtext: The reformation of a heel through the love of a good woman unfolds amid a family-like collection of European refugees waiting to enter America.

Background: In one early scene Brackett and Wilder had Georges talk to a cockroach in his hotel room about the frustration of waiting for a quota number. Charles Boyer thought the idea demeaning, and Mitchell Leisen placated the star by dropping the scene. Wilder was furious. He and Brackett wrote the last third of the movie to give as many of Boyer's lines as possible to Olivia de Havilland.

The Script: The script veers toward soap opera when a car crash, a chase across the border, a miraculous hospital recovery, and a reunion scene are all wedged into the final fifteen minutes. Most of the previous scenes, however, are strong. Georges' seduction of Emmy in the hotel lobby is especially well written. He uses the analogy of a schoolroom and chides her over sending every disobedient thought off to stand in a corner.

The Wilder Mensch: Hammock, the immigration officer, truly cares about the refugees at the hotel. His sternness in questioning Emmy about Georges' intentions is that of a protective guardian. Once he knows that Georges loves her, Hammock looks the other way after Georges illegally enters the US to reach Emmy, and he even finds Georges a job. The part is played by Walter Abel, who had the somewhat comparable role of Phillips in *Arise, My Love*.

Meaningful Objects: The wedding ring Georges gives Emmy reveals character. He borrows it from Anita but tells Emmy it belonged to his mother. Later, Anita asks Emmy to check the ring's inscription ("To Toots") as a confirmation of Georges' lies. Emmy refuses, but after she shields Georges from Hammock she removes the ring, again without reading the inscription, and leaves it on a table. Emmy's shy simplicity and sweetness are conveyed more through objects (her $500 of savings that she gives Georges; the wedding cake she brings him) than through her dialogue, a wise antidote to the sentimentality inherent in the story. Hearing a local legend that a child will be born for each olive that falls, Emmy treasures (and even names) the three olives that fall from the tree Georges shakes during the village festival honoring brides and bridegrooms. On their car trip, Emmy interprets the rhythm of the windshield wipers to be saying "together, together, together," a word that Georges later whispers to her at the hospital to bring her out of her coma.

The Visual Element: A nice touch appears during the car trip when Georges begins to regret his cruelty. Trying to stop his exploitation of Emmy, he pretends at a rest stop to have wrenched his shoulder. He sleeps sitting up in the front seat and thus keeps their marriage unconsummated. His glances in the rear-view mirror, however, of Emmy lovingly bedded down in the back only protract Georges' feelings of guilt.

The Verdict: Olivia de Havilland's subtle, sensitive performance rivals her work in *The Heiress*. The film is weakened, however, by Charles Boyer's wooden acting and the melodramatic resolution. *3/5*

Ball Of Fire (1941)

Director: Howard Hawks

Writers: Charles Brackett & Billy Wilder, based on a story by Wilder & Thomas Monroe

Cast: Gary Cooper (Bertram Potts), Barbara Stanwyck (Sugarpuss O'Shea), Oscar Homolka (Gurkakoff), Richard Haydn (Oddly), Henry Travers (Jerome), S Z Sakall (Megenbruch), Dana Andrews (Joe Lilac), Allen Jenkins (Garbage Man), Gene Krupa (Himself), 111 minutes

Story: Bertram Potts is one of eight lovable but stuffy professors sequestered at an estate to write an encyclopedia. Potts has spent three weeks finishing his entry on slang, but after listening to the colorful talk of his own garbage man, he decides that his article is already outdated. He ventures out to record the living speech of New Yorkers. Nightclub singer Sugarpuss O'Shea takes Potts' card and later arrives at the estate to hide out from the police who want to question her about her mobster boyfriend Joe Lilac. Over the next week her presence breathes life into the musty old house. Becoming fond of these quirky men, Sugar teaches the professors to conga and demonstrates to Potts' delight her meaning of "yum-yum" or kissing.

To Sugar such affection is simply a way of extending her visit and avoiding the police, but to Potts it means much more. With the encouragement of his seven colleagues, he buys an engagement ring and proposes to Sugar. His complete unpretentiousness disarms her, although she can see some problems. His annual salary equals the amount she spends on a pedicure.

In the meantime Joe Lilac has also proposed, wanting her as his wife to prevent her from testifying against him in court. Lilac telephones to order Sugar to his hideaway in New Jersey and intends for her to sneak past the police stake-out by having Potts and the professors drive her. On the trip, Professor Gurkakoff smashes into a road sign, and the party spends the night at a motel court while the car is repaired. That night Potts stumbles into Sugar's darkened room by mistake and, thinking he is talking to a colleague, he declares his feelings for Sugar. The next morning, Lilac and his men come to take her away, but now she realizes that she loves Bertram Potts. Even after returning to the hideout, Sugar refuses to marry Lilac.

The gangster sends two stooges to the estate to force Potts into convincing Sugar by telephone to agree to the wedding. The professors use their greater knowledge and their quick thinking to get the drop on the two hoods. The professors ride to New Jersey still in their cutaways and top hats and chauffeured by their pal the garbage man. They arrive just in time to prevent the wedding.

Subtext: To modify the famous description of *The Apartment,* this film is a non-dirty fairy tale for adults, or more exactly, a modern spin on *Snow White And The Seven Dwarfs.* Brackett and Wilder reverse the usual expectations by making the woman the cynical one who finds the integrity and innocence of Bertram Potts irresistible. Sugar's rejection of Lilac for Potts is made believable by the scriptwriters' refusal to have her resort to conventional romantic platitudes. Instead, in one of the film's many comic reversals, Sugar scolds herself as harshly as Lilac does for loving Potts, calling Potts a guy who "gets drunk on a glass of buttermilk … and doesn't know how to kiss." Her own amazement over loving Potts reinforces her resolve to spurn Lilac.

Background: Samuel Goldwyn, the head of his own independent studio, worked out a complicated trade with Paramount to obtain the services of Brackett and Wilder for his star Gary Cooper. Wilder showed Goldwyn a treatment of an idea that Goldwyn approved on his wife's recommendation (evidently not an uncommon practice for the language-mangling mogul). When Goldwyn haggled over the payment, Wilder sweetened his own deal by insisting on permission to observe Howard Hawks direct the film. Wilder was planning to pester Paramount into letting him direct as they had recently done for another successful writer, Preston Sturges. Wilder received an Oscar nomination for his story idea. Hawks also directed a musical remake in 1948 with Danny Kaye and Virginia Mayo. In the remake, *A Song Is Born,* slang is changed to jazz as the topic of the professors' research.

The Script: The script is a true gem of the screenwriting art, and it is hard to understand why Wilder has spoken indifferently of the film. Everything belongs. Even the recurrent business of opening the drapes delineates character and advances plot. After they are first opened, Potts confesses that he had to apply a wet cloth to his neck when he saw how beautiful Sugar looked in the sunlight. Needing more time to hide from the police, Sugar later deliberately positions herself in front of the window to catch the sun on her hair and thus distract Potts. The film climaxes when the professors aim a microscope's mirror to reflect the sunlight onto the cords supporting a portrait above Pastrami, the gangster holding them at gunpoint.

The film bristles with rich verbal touches and the lively ring of American slang. The screenplay lavishes care even on throwaway lines. An audience must listen attentively to mine all the gold. When the professors examine Sugar's sore throat, for example, she tells them, "It is as red as the *Daily Worker* and just as sore."

The Wilder Mensch: The comradely professors ("eight squirrelly cherubs," as Sugar calls them) and the garbage man support Potts' desire to propose, comfort him when he is rejected, and are probably among the few people who have treated Sugar decently.

Meaningful Objects: Rings advance the plot. Joe Lilac sends Sugar a diamond-studded engagement ring that makes Potts' $35 ring look scrawny. But as Sugar comes to love Potts, his ring is the one she prefers. She sends Lilac's ring to Potts with a note about breaking their engagement, an act that Gurkakoff, the psychology professor, explains by pointing out that subconsciously she is rejecting the ring she really doesn't want—Lilac's. He rightly interprets her gesture as an invitation for Potts to rescue her from Lilac.

The Visual Elements: Hawks directed in his usual classical, non-flashy manner. He clustered the professors in groups and de-emphasized editing so that the audience has many viewing options. Such directorial austerity—elegance but nothing too showy—also came to characterize the visual style of Wilder. Ed Sikov even claims that Wilder got more as a director from Hawks than from his idol Lubitsch, and Sikov is probably right (though Wilder said the opposite to Cameron Crowe).

At least in his early and middle periods, Lubitsch, like Hitchcock, favored stylistic touches that announced themselves whereas Wilder preferred a more transparent visual style. It would be a mistake to think that hiding the cinematic artistry does not usually require as much effort as calling attention to it.

The Verdict: Ball Of Fire appeared on the American Film Institute's list of the one hundred best comedies, a welcome surprise since it had been something of a neglected film. Today, its inventiveness seems to anticipate the postmodern fondness for rethinking classic stories in modern settings (*Emma* becoming *Clueless*; *The Taming Of The Shrew* becoming *Ten Things I Hate About You*). 5/5

"It's Not Necessary For A Director To Know How To Write; However, It Helps If He Knows How To Read"

Wilder's directing career grew out of his desire to see on screen the script that he and Charles Brackett had written. This early period proved to be one of the richest of his career. The films also reveal an attentive directorial eye. In 1945, Wilder served in the psychological warfare division of the American military; he used existing footage to supervise and edit the war department's information film, *Death Mills*, about the horrors of the concentration camps.

The Major And The Minor (1942)

Director: Billy Wilder
Writers: Charles Brackett & Billy Wilder, from the play *Connie Goes Home* by Edward Childs Carpenter, and a story by Fannie Kilbourne
Cast: Ginger Rogers (Susan Applegate), Ray Milland (Major Philip Kirby), Rita Johnson (Pamela), Diana Lynn (Lucy), Robert Benchley (Mr Osborne), Lela Rogers (Mrs Applegate), 101 minutes

Story: Susan Applegate has had twenty-five jobs during her year in New York. She quits working for a hair-care company after making an evening call on a Mr Osborne, a long-standing customer who clearly expects more than a scalp massage from his visitor. Susan has kept train fare for her return home to Stevenson, Iowa, but ticket prices have gone up. In her penniless desperation, she disguises herself as a twelve-year old to qualify for a child's fare. Two conductors suspect her ruse, and she runs into a stateroom to avoid being put off the train.

The stateroom belongs to Major Philip Kirby, the instructor at a boys' military school. Kirby's bad eye disqualifies him for active duty. The next morning Kirby's fiancée, Pamela, boards the train early and finds Susan still in the major's compartment. Kirby persuades Sue-Sue, as he calls Susan, to accompany him to his school to explain the appearance of a woman in his stateroom. Pamela and the faculty, seeing Susan in her little-girl outfit, accept the explanation, but Pamela's street-smart younger sister Lucy immediately sees through Susan's disguise. Lucy and Susan become friends since neither has much use for Pamela: Susan herself is attracted to Kirby, and Lucy resents the way Pamela has connived to keep Kirby inactive for military service. Lucy, who plans to be a scientist, infuriates her sister by using Pamela's crystal wedding bowl to house a tadpole. The girls outsmart Pamela and obtain for Kirby his commission. At a school dance, one of the cadets' fathers turns out to be Mr Osborne, the man with the dry scalp from New York. He reveals Susan to Pamela, who uses her knowledge to blackmail Susan into leaving the school.

Back in Stevenson, Susan's mother gets a call from Kirby. He has been transferred to active duty and will stop by on his way to San Diego. Susan decides to welcome him disguised as her mother. Kirby reports that Pamela wed someone else and that his train will later stop at Las Vegas, where couples can get married in five minutes. After sending him off to the depot, Susan meets him there, dressed as herself.

Subtext: In its overall structure, the film plays coyly with a subtext of paedophilia, but in its development this *Lolita* theme is not really exploited. Kirby always treats Sue-Sue with exaggerated avuncular politeness, and his deeper attraction to her seems to occur without his entirely realizing it. The best scenes nevertheless work on more than one level and generate a comic tension through Susan's pleasant discomfort over recognizing, along with the audience, that Kirby desires her. The well-done final scene resolves this courtship-in-the-making without ever really spelling out for Kirby quite what has gone on.

Background: Wilder wanted to make the most popular movie he could to calm front-office fears that he would flop as a novice director by undertaking some overly ambitious drama. He made a good choice, perhaps desiring to continue the playful tone of *Ball Of Fire.* The trailer for this film announced it as 'a bedtime story for grown-up children.' Ginger Rogers' mother in the film is played by her real-life mother. The film was remade as a Dean Martin and Jerry Lewis vehicle (with Jerry in the Ginger Rogers part), *You're Never Too Young* (1955). Diana Lynn also appeared in that film.

The Script: This may be the only romantic comedy that ends with a 'meet cute.' In the final scene at the depot, Brackett and Wilder wisely avoid the expected, 'on the nose' approach. The audience has been wondering how Kirby and Susan will handle the obligatory 'It was you all along' scene. The writers solve the problem by simply making the scene non-obligatory. Susan, who has fooled Kirby by disguising herself both as Sue-Sue and as her own mother, now greets him as herself. She frankly tells him that she is headed to Las Vegas to marry a soldier and then kisses him by using the same make-out ruse that the cadets had earlier tried on her.

The comedy of confused identities in the train compartment anticipates the later scene in the upper berth between Jack Lemmon and Marilyn Monroe in *Some Like It Hot.* Brackett and Wilder pepper the script with some clever in-jokes: playful references to Greta Garbo and Veronica Lake, a swipe at Charles Boyer.

The Wilder Mensch: The smart, no-nonsense Lucy keeps the cuteness of the film from becoming cloying. She teaches Susan the 23 musts and 24 must-nots of life at the military school. She keeps Susan in cigarettes, which Susan playfully lights from Lucy's Bunsen burner. Most important, Lucy tells Susan about Pamela's plot to keep Kirby from active duty. The girls commandeer the switchboard and place a long-distance call to Washington to negate Pamela's scheme. (This scene, in which Ginger Rogers coaxes the cadet on switchboard duty away from his post with a fetching tap-dance, is one of the film's highlights.) The most directly honest line in the script is Lucy's confession to Susan that she is more her sister than Pamela ever was.

Meaningful Objects: When Major Kirby arrives at Susan's home in Iowa he brings a present from Lucy—a jar with the frog that Lucy's tadpole has finally become. Kirby will soon find when he gets to the train station that Sue-Sue has similarly transformed herself, Gigi-like, into a fully grown woman. Moths and butterflies, tadpoles and frogs underline the film's comic theme of transformation.

The Visual Element: Wilder's first solo effort at directing looks very assured. The brief montage of Ginger Rogers in the ladies' lounge adapting the contents of her suitcase into little girl's attire may be unneeded, however. Later, in *Some Like It Hot,* Wilder cuts directly from Jack Lemmon and Tony Curtis deciding to disguise themselves as women to a shot of them in drag walking to their train. The audience simply accepts that they somehow solved all the problems in creating the disguise.

When Sue-Sue first enters the mess hall, Wilder italicizes the moment with a nicely done tracking shot of lines of cadets turning their heads to notice her. A similar moment occurs later when Miss Shackleford brings the girls from her school to the cadets' dance. One of the cadets tells Sue-Sue about the epidemic at Miss Shackleford's school. All of the girls, including their headmistress, have come down with Veronica Lake symptoms. Sue-Sue looks in puzzlement at the long perspective of girls waiting to dance and sees that they all have the peekaboo hair style of the famous Forties star.

Perhaps the subtlest visual touch comes when Susan returns to Stevenson, Iowa. She sits on the front porch with her home-town beau. Wilder pans to a close-up of the porch light with moths fluttering around it, and then cuts to a shot of a serene Susan watching them. Wordlessly, this sequence permits us to read her mind and know that she is recalling the analogy of moths and light bulbs Major Kirby used to caution Sue-Sue about the cadets' attraction to her. It was the first time Kirby revealed his own awareness of her appeal. With these two shots we see that Susan's mind and heart are still back at the school with Kirby.

The Verdict: The early scenes buying the train ticket and eluding the conductors may slow the pace somewhat, but everything else works beautifully. *4/5*

Five Graves To Cairo (1943)

Director: Billy Wilder
Writers: Charles Brackett & Billy Wilder, from the play *Hotel Imperial* by Lajos Biro
Cast: Franchot Tone (Bramble), Anne Baxter (Mouche), Akim Tamiroff (Farid), Erich von Stroheim (Rommel), Peter Van Eyck (Schwegler), Fortunio Bonanova (Sebastiano), Miles Mander (Colonel Fitzhume), 97 minutes

Story: A tank of corpses rolls across the desert of North Africa. One near-dead British soldier tumbles out of the tank turret and onto the sand. He staggers to Sidi Halfaya, an evacuated village, and to the Empress Of Britain hotel. He is only minutes ahead of the advancing Germans, who have routed the British Eighth Army at Tobruk. This soldier, J J Bramble, is tended to by the Egyptian hotel manager Farid and the French chambermaid Mouche. Before the famous Desert Fox Rommel arrives, his advance troops, led by Lieutenant Schwegler, prepare the way. Coldly efficient, Schwegler confirms details about Farid and Mouche by consulting a small notebook. Farid and Mouche marvel at his knowledge about them. Meanwhile, Bramble dresses himself upstairs in the clothes of Davos, the hotel's club-footed waiter recently killed in an air raid.

When Rommel arrives, Bramble sees from his treatment that Davos was really a German spy supplying the advance information about Farid and Mouche to the Nazis. A group of captured British officers is brought in. Rommel can't resist giving them the chance at dinner to question him about his brilliance in maintaining his supply lines. He tells them that the secret is not in bringing supplies to the men but in taking the men to the supplies. He refuses, however, to reveal the location of the German provisions and ammunition buried in the Egyptian desert; later Bramble stares at Rommel's map of Egypt trying to discern their location. With a tip from Farid, Bramble suddenly realizes the clever positions of the 'five graves to Cairo' and traces their sites on a piece of mosquito netting placed over the map.

During an air raid, Lieutenant Schwegler finds the corpse of the real Davos in the cellar. Bramble must kill Schwegler to maintain his disguise.

33

He places the body in Mouche's bed to divert suspicion from himself. He plans to leave later for Cairo on Davos' next mission, and he gives proof to Farid that will clear Mouche from suspicion in Schwegler's murder. Rommel begins his interrogation of Mouche as Bramble departs to alert the British about the location of the German ammunition supplies. Months later, after Rommel's defeat at El Alamein, Bramble returns to the Empress Of Britain. Farid tells him the tragic news. Though he produced evidence to clear Mouche, the Germans nonetheless beat her to death.

Subtext: The developing story concerns duty, sacrifice, and the cat-and-mouse game of outsmarting a cunning enemy. Wilder's fondness for disguise and deception also permeates the film. Mouche seems ready to trade sex with Schwegler for softer treatment from the Nazis, but she is really intent on obtaining the release of her brother.

Background: It was Lajos Biro, reportedly, who suggested that his World War I play *Hotel Imperial* could be updated to fit the current world situation. The play had been unsatisfactorily filmed twice before, once as a silent film and again in 1939 as a vehicle for Ray Milland. The date on Brackett and Wilder's completed shooting script, 17 December 1942, was just one month after the defeat of Rommel in North Africa. The film was released in theaters in May 1943. Wilder's respect and admiration for Stroheim as a director was second only to his affection for his idol, Ernst Lubitsch. The part of Rommel is a larger-than-life role wonderfully played by Stroheim. Wilder biographer Kevin Lally reports that Cary Grant was originally sought for the Franchot Tone part. Grant balked over the time required for location shooting in the Arizona desert. The film marked the first collaboration between Wilder and composer Miklós Rózsa.

The Script: The script is one of Brackett and Wilder's best. They wisely downplay the melodrama of the plot by having Rommel call attention to it himself in his first scene with Mouche after she pleads for the release of her brother ("This is a familiar scene, reminiscent of bad melodrama"). His stylized but deflating speech which follows exploits the tension of the moment by seeming to undercut it.

The script also gains a rhythmic snap through some verbal repetitions. Bramble, dressed as the waiter/spy Davos, says that he is "the vulture who flies ahead of the Stukkas," winning rare praise from Rommel: "Rather well said." A few moments later, when Rommel colorfully describes the Nazis' plans for subduing Churchill, Bramble curtly repeats this three-word commendation to the field marshal, a flourish that earns more of Rommel's trust. In another example, Rommel rudely distances Mouche ("Two steps back") when she serves him breakfast in bed; in the later interrogation scene, she shows her defiance by repeating these same words to him as he advances toward her.

The exposition, in particular, shows great finesse. Bramble's hallucinations from sun stroke in the hotel lobby not only add a touch of the macabre but also supply the audience with antecedent information about his involvement in the British defeat in North Africa. He makes such a ghostly spectacle talking to imaginary officers that Farid and Mouche must tend to him, a transition that incorporates these new characters dramatically and visually into the film with great smoothness. (They appear initially in long shots as background figures who stop their work to stare at the soldier talking to empty air.)

The Wilder Mensch: Mouche's integrity and determination encourage and inspire Bramble. Making the character of conscience a victim of the Germans heightens the seriousness of the drama. Farid is smart enough to know when to play the fool to the Germans, but he comes to care for the welfare of Mouche and Bramble. Farid also helps Bramble crack the map code by showing him the 1930s photograph of Rommel in Egypt disguised as an archeology professor.

Meaningful Objects: The mystery of the map becomes a plot-fueling device, a MacGuffin in the fashion of most Hitchcock films. Other props personalize characters. Rommel carries a 'fly-swisher' (according to the shooting script) that he waves imperiously like a riding crop. Arthur Lennig, the author of a 2000 biography of Stroheim, writes that the actor himself may have suggested the business of slapping Mouche with the swatter during the interrogation scene. ('Mouche,' by the way, is French for 'fly.') In another example, Mouche shows Bramble a white dress she bought in Paris but laments not having been able to afford the matching ivory-handled parasol. Bramble later buys the parasol for her. He brings it with him when he returns with the British to liberate Sidi Halfaya. After hearing from Farid that Mouche is dead, Bramble uses the parasol to shade her grave as he delivers a patriotic speech similar to Joel McCrea's words at the end of Hitchcock's *Foreign Correspondent*.

The Visual Element: John Seitz, working in his first of four films with Wilder, was deservedly nominated for an Oscar. The film is shot mostly in high-contrast or low-key lighting, a strategy that creates some richly atmospheric moments. In one, Bramble prepares for sleep and Mouche moves the ceiling light to a position behind her dressing screen. Immediately the texture of the room light darkens, inducing the reverie that follows between Bramble and Mouche as they stretch out on their separate cots with the screen between them. In another effective moment, Wilder shoots the fight between Bramble and Schwegler with the unmoving camera trained only on a dropped flashlight. The sounds of the scuffle occur in complete darkness except for this small circle of light. After two pistol shots, the victor retrieves the torch, and the beam passes briefly over the dead face of Schwegler. It is a stylishly understated way of revealing the struggle and its outcome.

Stroheim's introduction is another virtuoso touch. In a point of view shot from a balcony, we see his back while he paces and barks out communiqués to Berlin. Wilder has often said that Stroheim's thick neck was more expressive than some actors' faces. Stroheim's image is dramatically checkered by the shadows cast by the blades of a rotating ceiling fan. We see his face in close-up only at the moment when he completes his messages and turns to dictate his name. Wilder also uses two matching camera moves to great effect. The excellent opening scene concludes with the camera slowly zooming in to the dog tags on the unconscious soldier. We can read the name of the protagonist, J J Bramble. Later, when Bramble wants silently to reassure the captured British officers that he too is British, he wraps the same tags around a decanter of whiskey on his serving tray. The camera moves in to pick out this detail at the same time it is recognized by the senior officer.

The Verdict: Strengthened by a great performance by Stroheim, *Five Graves To Cairo* is Wilder's most underrated film. *4/5*

Double Indemnity (1944)

Director: Billy Wilder
Writers: Billy Wilder & Raymond Chandler, from the novel by James M Cain
Cast: Fred MacMurray (Walter Neff), Barbara Stanwyck (Phyllis Dietrichson), Edward G Robinson (Barton Keyes), Porter Hall (Mr Jackson), Jean Heather (Lola Dietrichson), Tom Powers (Mr Dietrichson), Byron Barr (Nino Zachetti), Richard Gaines (Mr Norton), 107 minutes

Story: Dying from a gunshot wound, Walter Neff confesses a murder to his boss Barton Keyes on an office Dictaphone. His story begins a few months ago. Neff, an insurance salesman for Pacific All-Risk, dropped in at the Dietrichson house to renew some automobile policies. Phyllis Dietrichson was alone. As Neff flirted with Phyllis, she inquired about accident insurance and hinted at a desire to murder her husband. When Phyllis later showed up at Neff's apartment, he agreed to help her pull it off. They secretly took out an accident policy with a double indemnity clause on the husband—twice the death benefit if the insured died in a train accident. Neff carefully planned and carried out the murder so that

36

Dietrichson appeared to have broken his neck in a fall from the back of a train.

Eventually, Keyes, the claims manager, became suspicious of Phyllis and some unknown accomplice. Dietrichson's daughter Lola visited Neff with the same concern. She told Neff that she also suspected Phyllis of having murdered her mother, the first Mrs Dietrichson, in order to marry her father. Soon both Keyes and Lola suspected Phyllis' co-conspirator to be Nino Zachetti, Lola's ex-boyfriend. Neff saw a way out. He planned to kill Phyllis and frame Zachetti. However, on his late-night visit Phyllis shot Neff first in the shoulder. When she could not finish the job, Neff shot Phyllis twice at close range and drove to his office to confess.

Before he finishes, Keyes arrives. Neff wants to make it across the border, but he collapses before he can get to the elevator.

Subtext: The quintessential film noir is strengthened by a father-son relationship between Keyes and Neff that nearly rivals for centrality in the film the romantic one between Neff and Phyllis.

Background: Wilder first came across James M Cain's short novel when he noticed a secretary at Paramount absent from her desk. She was in the ladies' room finishing Cain's book, which was sufficient recommendation of its quality for Brackett and Wilder. Charles Brackett, however, soon left the project because of the sordid subject matter. Since Cain was unavailable, Wilder asked hard-boiled detective novelist Raymond Chandler to collaborate. Their rocky association produced the classic screenplay that appears today in the Library of America series of classic texts.

Wilder had to wheedle and cajole Fred MacMurray, who had established himself in light comedy, to accept the part of Walter Neff. MacMurray explained years later that his hesitation had less to do with the fear of disappointing his loyal fans than with his own uncertainties about being equal to the demands of the role. Of MacMurray's 85 films, his two performances for Wilder (here and in *The Apartment*) are the most memorable. A concluding scene was filmed but not used in which Keyes watches Neff die in the gas chamber.

The Script: The dialogue has become rightly regarded as some of the most memorable in American movies. The use of metaphor enriches the film's slang. As Richard Armstrong points out, Neff's flirtatious talk is both chided and encouraged by Phyllis through the conceit of a speeding ticket ("How fast was I going, officer?"). Planning murder and an insurance swindle, Neff compares himself to a croupier who knows all the notches on the roulette wheel and who only needs the right shill to "crook the house." Keyes delivers a bravura rebuke to the big boss Norton by comparing Norton's botched meeting with Phyllis to a series of setbacks on the football field. Another sustained metaphor is the repeated trolley-car references to describe the way murder inevitably requires its participants to ride "straight down the line." Neff's street slang fits his hard-edged personality. He refers variously to "a morgue job" and "a monoxide job," the vernacular of someone who seems never to have quite fitted in.

The short scene in Norton's office is a good example of the consistent strengths of the script. The banter between Norton and Keyes over the Dietrichson claim establishes tension. The editing inserts reaction shots of Neff and Phyllis to punctuate with visual asides Norton's speculations about the case. Best of all, Keyes demolishes Norton's theory that Dietrichson committed suicide, thus unknowingly assisting the killers. The scene rigorously avoids the obvious, exploits suspense, and creates a rich subtext.

The Wilder Mensch: Barton Keyes has "a little man" inside him who ties his stomach in knots every time a fake claim crosses his desk. In his monograph on the film for the BFI, Richard Schickel identifies the fuller development of Keyes from the novel to the film as one of the screenwriters' chief creative insights. Keyes tears into Norton's theory of suicide in an aria-like spiel. He cites statistics from actuarial tables as if they were sacred texts. But he is also a man whose integrity and dedication to work have made him lonely. At one point Keyes offers Neff a job as his assistant, and his eagerness implies that his bond with Walter is the closest one he has. Neff too realizes that "behind the cigar ashes on his vest" Keyes has "a heart as big as a house." Emotionally, Neff's betrayal of Keyes rivals his other crimes.

Meaningful Objects: The first close shot of Phyllis singles out her anklet as she descends the stairs. Her cheap appeal is suggested by the anklet and the nameless perfume she bought in Ensenada. Seedy locations—Jerry's Market, a bowling alley, a drive-in burger joint—also capture the feeling of California decay.

The Visual Element: What came to be known as the elements of film noir provide atmosphere: dark urban streets, low-keyed lighting. Director of photography John Seitz used aluminum filings to catch the sunlight and serve as dust motes when Neff visits the Dietrichson house.

The Verdict: Billy Wilder's first masterpiece. 5/5

The Lost Weekend (1945)

Director: Billy Wilder
Writers: Charles Brackett & Billy Wilder, based on the novel by Charles R Jackson
Cast: Ray Milland (Don Birnam), Jane Wyman (Helen St James), Phillip Terry (Wick Birnam), Howard Da Silva (Nat the Bartender), Doris Dowling (Gloria), Frank Faylen (Bim), 101 minutes

Story: Unemployed Don Birnam, a novelist manqué, packs for a weekend in the country with his brother Wick, but his mind is really on the bottle he has hidden outside his bedroom window. Don's girlfriend Helen arrives to say goodbye, and Wick spots and confiscates Don's bottle. Don decides to take a later train to the country so he can be alone for a while. Using money Wick has hidden to pay the cleaning lady, Don goes to Nat's Bar for another "jigger of dreams." He jokes with Nat and Gloria, a prostitute who has a crush on him. Don tells Nat about his plans for an autobiographical novel. It will relate how he met Helen three years ago when their claim checks got switched at the cloakroom of the Metropolitan Opera. Don's binge of drinking and storytelling makes him miss his train. During his long weekend, Don tries to hock his typewriter for drinking money, to steal a woman's purse at a supper club, and to survive a bout of DTs after a night in the drunk ward at Bellevue Hospital. Finally, he reclaims a revolver he once pawned. Helen, arriving Monday to check on Don, sees the hidden gun in Don's bathroom and distracts him from suicide by offering him drinks. Eventually, Nat arrives with Don's typewriter and another chance to start his book. With Helen's encouragement, Don decides to channel his frustration into a novel and even to begin it with the events of that very weekend, when he was packing his suitcase with his mind on the bottle outside the window.

Subtext: The first close-up of Don Birnam is played like a trump at bridge, one of the director's favorite games. It comes when Don's emotions awaken as he has a drink at Nat's and begins to soliloquize about the power of alcohol. His florid speech (Leslie Halliwell reprints it in his *Film Guide*) suggests that this novelist loves drink because of the creative assist it provides. Later, however, in the scene when Don first tells Helen about his drinking, we hear the self-disgust and sunken esteem behind the poetic veneer. The film explores the contrast between the charming writer Don seems and the weak failure he believes himself to be. It is in many ways a film about weakness—Don's weakness with the bottle and Helen's weakness in loving Don. One moving moment occurs when even the cynical prostitute Gloria abandons her anger over being stood up by Don and tells him softly, "I waited half the night like it was the first date I ever had." Her desperation and weakness appear just below her hard surface.

Background: Wilder himself initiated the project after reading Charles Jackson's novel on a cross-country train trip. Though it was perceived as a groundbreaking film from the start, he may have also been attracted to the book because the main character is a writer, someone with whom Wilder could identify. His films feature a number of other writer-protagonists: screenwriter Joe Gillis (in *Sunset Boulevard)*, journalist Chuck Tatum (in *Ace In The Hole),* and the newsmen in *The Front Page.* Paramount studio head Buddy De Sylva convinced Wilder of the wisdom of accepting a personality star in the lead for this hard-hitting film rather than a more established dramatic actor.

Ray Milland experienced the same worries about meeting the challenges of the role that had bothered Fred MacMurray in undertaking *Double Indemnity.* But charm is one of Don Birnam's key traits, and Milland's likable screen persona works to great advantage in the film. Brackett and Wilder had to mollify the liquor industry that the film was primarily a case study rather than a plea for temperance. Some of the scenes—Milland's long walk down Third Avenue, his weary climb to board the elevated train, the shot of him leaving Bellevue Hospital—were filmed at the actual locations with concealed cameras. The film was badly received by a preview audience. Wilder biographer Kevin Lally speculates that an inferior musical score was the cause. Miklós Rózsa replaced it with the now-familiar, Oscar-nominated score that prominently features the theremin, an electronic instrument capable of the haunting tremolos that Rózsa also incorporated into his famous score for Hitchcock's *Spellbound.*

The Script: For the second film in a row, Wilder received perhaps the highest compliment he could from the author of the source material. Charles Jackson, like James M Cain after seeing *Double Indemnity,* praised the finished film by saying that Brackett and Wilder had come up with touches for the movie that he wished he had thought of for his novel. Nearly every scene succeeds on more than one level. Don's schemes to delay his trip to the country, for example, affirm his cleverness, dramatize his desperation, and begin to alienate Wick and Helen. The script's natural movement toward tragedy is averted at the end, an artistic choice some have faulted.

The Wilder Mensch: At first, Helen and Wick are the most vocal representation of Don's conscience, but their good intentions have a softness that sometimes appears as excuse-making. Unconsciously, they may provide an element of "enabling" for Don, as the current psychological term labels it. Wick even goes so far as to pretend to be the family drinker to quell Helen's suspicions about Don. The film's real voice of conscience and tough love appears unexpectedly in Nat the Bartender, who also illustrates Wilder's love of paradox. This bartender knows from experience what years of later therapy have confirmed: that a drinker first has to want to become sober more than anything else. Nat alternately serves Don drinks and scolds him for his mistreatment of both Helen and Gloria. In one chilling moment, Nat even predicts the inevitability of Don's suicide with a dismissive snap of his fingers. This bluntness becomes therapeutic, however, driving Don back to his typewriter to make another start on his novel. The final impetus toward life and away from suicide also comes courtesy of Nat, when he returns Don's typewriter to him at his apartment. It is the only time Nat appears away from his bar. (Compare Nat to the sadistic Bim, the night nurse at Bellevue and another person who treats Don roughly, and Nat's essential life-affirming nature becomes even clearer.)

Meaningful Objects: The pattern of concentric shot-glass rings on the bar top ("Don't wipe it away, Nat") logs the depth of Don's drunkenness. The film also has a circular structure, ending with a reversal of the image with which it begins, a slow pan across a skyline to Don's bottle hanging from a rope out of his window as he packs for the weekend. The exchanged coats at the cloakroom afford Don and Helen an excuse to meet, and when he later trades her leopard coat at the hock shop for his revolver, she interprets the grim symbolism for him. Brackett and Wilder concisely focus most of Don's behavior around two defining objects that compete for his attention and his soul: his hidden bottles and his typewriter.

The Visual Element: Visually, it is one of Wilder's most impressive films. The malicious wit and the effective editing of Don at the opera sweating his way through the drinking song of *La Traviata* is worthy of Hitchcock, who liked to explain in interviews the power of such constructive editing. Showing a shot of a character looking, a shot of what the character sees, and a shot of his reaction invites the audience to construct the character's feelings. Thus a film-maker can develop character pictorially through montage. Wilder paces this scene perfectly. The camera notes each raised glass and iced bottle, images followed by shots of Don's increasing discomfort. Eventually, the line of performers on stage in period costume transforms expressionistically into a row of raincoats like the one in which Don has hidden a bottle in the cloakroom.

At an opposite visual extreme, some lengthy, deep-focus shots position characters in a layered depth of field that provides the audience with the chance to choose details and, in effect, edit the scene themselves. When

Don calls Helen from the lobby phone at the hotel, for example, we see her take the call in the distant background and slump in disappointment as he lies to her about being unable to meet her parents.

The Verdict: The film won Oscars for best picture, director, screenplay, and actor. It was also nominated for best cinematography, editing, and score. The many capsule reviewers (Mick Martin, Leslie Halliwell) who claim that the film has lost none of its punch do not exaggerate. 5/5

The Emperor Waltz (1948)

Director: Billy Wilder
Writers: Charles Brackett & Billy Wilder
Cast: Bing Crosby (Virgil Smith), Joan Fontaine (Countess Johanna), Richard Haydn (The Emperor Franz Josef), Roland Culver (The Baron), Lucile Watson (Princess Bitotska), Sig Ruman (Dr Zwieback the veterinarian), 106 minutes

Story: On a wintry evening around 1906 at the Viennese palace of the Emperor Franz Josef, an American traveling salesman, Virgil Smith, crashes a formal ball. He and the Countess Johanna trade insults on the dance floor but go off waltzing together. Four surprised onlookers review the background of this relationship. Virgil and the countess met months before when their dogs skirmished outside the palace. Virgil was seeking an audience with the emperor to solicit his endorsement for a phonograph; Johanna and her father were there to agree to a match between their pedigreed Scheherazade and the emperor's poodle.

The action moves to the emperor's hunting lodge in the Tyrol where Johanna discovers that Scheherazade, after two scraps with Virgil's fox-terrier, Buttons, now is fearful of all dogs. The court veterinarian, a disciple of Freud, prescribes a friendly canine meeting to relax Scheherazade. As the two dogs settle their differences, Virgil and Johanna also fall in love. When Virgil asks the emperor for Johanna's hand in marriage, Franz Josef points out the multitude of problems caused by their class barriers. Nobly, Virgil relents, lying to Johanna that he only pretended to love her in order to gain the emperor's approval for his phonograph.

Back at the palace on the night of the ball, Virgil again confronts Johanna, telling her that Buttons is sick without his mate. Scheherazade, however, is about to have her litter. The emperor and Johanna's father pace nervously in the royal kennel as Virgil and Buttons observe through a frosty window. It turns out that the puppies are not the dark pure-bred poodles everyone expects but three white mutts resembling Buttons. The baron, Johanna's father, is furious. "That blasted, black Jezebel!" he says about Scheherazade (a line the censor changed from "that blasted, black bitch"). The baron tries to spare the emperor's disappointment by telling

42

him that the dogs were born dead. Before the vet can do away with them, however, Virgil comes to the pups' rescue. He presents them to the emperor, who finds them quite appealing. Virgil and Johanna now reconcile.

Subtext: The film explores the clash between the declining old world aristocracy of the Austro-Hungarian empire and the rising modern age. This serious-sounding conflict plays out in the improbable world of musical comedy. Scott Eyman, the biographer of Ernst Lubitsch, reports (as do Wilder's two most recent biographers) that the idea of using the mutual attraction and rutting of two dogs as a parallel for the growing love affair of their owners was one Wilder borrowed from Lubitsch. It is the film's most inventive touch (and a later source of irritation to Lubitsch when he saw his idea popping up in somebody else's movie). Another key Wilder element in this post-World War II movie is the business of drowning the mongrel puppies. In this scene the camera records a surprising level of detail for such an airy film: the German veterinarian, grimly following the baron's orders for a canine final solution, has his assistant cover the head of Scheherazade while he gathers her puppies into a wire basket, carries it to a sink, and turns on the water.

Background: Paramount wanted its two hottest writers to come up with a vehicle for its top star, but all the Tyrolean effervescence gets smothered by the heavy schmaltz of Bing Crosby. In one scene Bing strolls along an alpine pass and sings with his own echo. Milkmaids start to yodel. Men on a passing hay wain join in. The love plot becomes the biggest loser. Dorothy Lamour made an apt comment about Crosby for a documentary on the singer. Quoting a telling lyric from his hit song 'Moonlight Becomes You' ('If I say I love you, I want you to know....'), Lamour emphasized the importance of the first word 'if.' Crosby's on-screen appeal, she contended, was essentially that of a loner. If the obligatory love scenes in his films could be softened or, better yet, implied, his character benefited.

The Script: The script for *The Emperor Waltz* is one of Wilder's few that probably reads better than it plays. The flashback structure with the four gossiping courtiers works well. Dressed in elegant attire, they watch the couples at the royal palace waltz by and kibbutz about them like bleacher bums at a baseball park ("The La Fuentes have more of everything; in fact, most of their children were born with eleven fingers"). The ringleader is the dowager Princess Bitotska, whose withering rebukes always bring the film to life.

The flavor of Brackett and Wilder's best work comes out in two exceptional speeches. In the first, Virgil segues into a song by flattering Johanna and comparing her to a beautiful chandelier. Later, the emperor explains to Virgil the obsolescence of the elite by comparing them to snails: "They are majestic creatures with small coroneted heads that peer very proudly from their tiny castles. They move with dignity. I imagine they have a great sense of their own importance, but you take them from their shells and they die. That is us, Mr. Smith." Both images make the same point about form superseding function. The chandelier countess, thanks to her love and youth, can adapt, but the snail-like, aged emperor can only look to a diminished future and death.

The Wilder Mensch: The two dogs bring Virgil and Johanna together; their puppies reunite them.

Meaningful Objects: The phonograph heralds the coming modern age. Virgil sets his machine blaring in the woods to get the emperor's attention, and he orders Buttons to strike a pose in front of the horn resembling the RCA trademark. After delivering his speech about snails, the emperor tiredly turns to Virgil for a demonstration of his strange-looking contraption. It's the old world reluctantly accepting its decline.

The Visual Element: The Technicolor photography and Edith Head's Oscar-nominated costumes for Joan Fontaine seem to have received all the visual attention. Wilder was later to say that the over-lush color even made the dialogue sound bad.

The Verdict: The roles of the baron and the emperor are wonderfully played by Roland Culver and Richard Haydn, but the leads have no chemistry. *2/5*

A Foreign Affair (1948)

Director: Billy Wilder
Writers: Charles Brackett, Billy Wilder & Richard L Breen, based on a screen story by David & Irwin Shaw
Cast: Jean Arthur (Phoebe Frost), Marlene Dietrich (Erika von Schlüetow), John Lund (Colonel John Pringle), Millard Mitchell (Colonel Rufus Plummer), Peter von Zerneck (Hans Otto Birgel), 116 minutes

Story: A US congressional committee has come to post-war Berlin to investigate the questionable conduct of American soldiers or, as congresswoman Phoebe Frost calls it, their "moral malaria." She tracks down fellow Iowan Colonel John Pringle, the recipient of the birthday cake that Pringle's girlfriend, one of her constituents, asked Phoebe to deliver. Just because Pringle wears a uniform, however, doesn't make him a boy scout. He has been secretly keeping as his mistress Erika von Schlüetow, a chanteuse with ties to many former Nazis, especially Hans Otto Birgel, rumored still to be in hiding.

Phoebe hears Erika sing at a local cabaret, investigates her, and then unsuspectingly recruits Pringle to help her find the American soldier shielding Erika. To deflect her suspicions, Pringle pretends an attraction to Phoebe, and the proper, buttoned-down congresswoman responds. A jealous Erika eventually tells Phoebe about her relationship with Pringle. The American brass has known about it too and looked the other way in the hope that the affair would bring Birgel out of hiding. Colonel Plummer orders Pringle, who now discovers that he loves Phoebe, to continue seeing Erika. A round of gunfire in the darkened cabaret results in the capture of Birgel, and a worried Phoebe reconciles with Pringle.

Subtext: This is Billy Wilder's *Arms And The Man.* Just as Shaw's comedy applies a realistic eye to war and love, so too does Wilder's film. And both play and film eventually favor a 'both/and' view of their subjects rather than the 'either/or' approach one might expect. Such ambiguity is satisfying. Wilder finds in Erika's self-preservation a humanizing resilience, and under the cold, disapproving exterior of Phoebe Frost, he sees timidity and the hunger for love.

Background: The film was somewhat controversial because of its realistic picture of servicemen. Charles Brackett balked over what he perceived as the unpatriotic tone of the film. Jean Arthur, aged 42, had been away from Hollywood attending Stephens College in Columbia, Missouri, when she was offered the part. She had not made a film in three years and would only appear in one more, *Shane.* Always a very self-conscious performer, Arthur felt her insecurities mount when the glamorous Dietrich arrived. A few years before her death in 1991, Jean Arthur saw the film on television and loved it. She called Wilder to ask his forgiveness for the friction she had caused during filming. Hellmuth Karasek writes that Wilder returned her charity, saying that no apology was necessary.

The Script: It is one of Wilder's very best. The two cabaret scenes, for example, clearly mark the before-and-after extremes of Phoebe Frost in love. The introduction of Phoebe is also a treat. This emotionally closed congresswoman refuses to leave her airplane seat to view the rubble of Berlin until she punctiliously closes her notebook, caps her pen, folds her eyeglasses, zips her keyholder, and clasps her purse. Any movie scene that serves more than one purpose is effective; the classic file-room scene accomplishes at least three in a sly blend of comedy and drama that reveals Pringle's shrewdness and Phoebe's vulnerability.

The Wilder Mensch: Colonel Plummer is one of the most interesting and likable minor characters in Wilder's films. He also illustrates the film's healthy ambiguity. Plummer never fails to understand his military duty, but he is too involved with post-war reality to be idealistic. His non-judgmental view of GI behavior emerges in one early scene. Plummer delivers a monologue about the fall of the Nazis as he rides through bombed-out Berlin with the congressional committee. All around the city, of course, American soldiers are openly seducing German women. While Plummer blithely ignores the impropriety, close-ups of Phoebe register her shock at the sight of a woman pushing a baby carriage adorned with two small American flags. The dialogue of the scene thus delivers the official military viewpoint while the edited montage undercuts it with a picture of the actual reality. The film and Phoebe come around to Plummer's view. It is also Plummer who delays Phoebe's flight back to Washington so that she can discover for herself the importance of Pringle's hazardous mission.

Meaningful Objects: The emphasis on trading dramatizes the priorities of the characters. At the black market Pringle swaps the birthday cake Phoebe brought him for the more practical mattress he takes to Erika. As Pringle drives through the rubble of Berlin with the mattress rolled up in his jeep, he whistles 'Isn't It Romantic.' Later, Phoebe trades her typewriter at the same black market for the evening gown she wears for her night out with Pringle. The gown is too big for her, however, and the prim Republican has the bodice cinched up nearly to her chin. Pringle performs an adjustment.

The Visual Element: Some of Wilder's richest, most moving uses of *mise en scène* appear in this film. When Erika sings 'Illusions' at the cabaret, she strolls to Pringle and Phoebe's table. The camera captures them all—and their many mixed emotions—in the smoky, textured light. Erika is seen in the reflection of the glass behind the tables, and a violinist is added to enrich further the arrangement of objects. Another mirror shot comes when Pringle later returns to Erika's rooms. After he kisses Erika, he glimpses the reflection of Phoebe, who observes them in hiding. Wilder then cuts to a silhouette of Phoebe in profile with Charles Lang's camera catching the shimmer of her single tear.

The Verdict: The final pairing of Pringle and Phoebe may strain credulity a bit, but the film is an underrated gem in all other respects. *4/5*

Sunset Boulevard (1950)

Director: Billy Wilder
Writers: Charles Brackett, Billy Wilder & D M Marshman, Jr.
Cast: William Holden (Joe Gillis), Gloria Swanson (Norma Desmond), Erich von Stroheim (Max von Mayerling), Nancy Olson (Betty Shaefer), Fred Clark (Sheldrake), Jack Webb (Artie Green), Cecil B DeMille (Himself), Hedda Hopper (Herself), Buster Keaton (Himself), 110 minutes

Story: There's a body in the pool. It belongs to Joe Gillis, a screenwriter "with a couple of B pictures to his credit." As flashbulbs pop while the homicide squad fishes him out, Joe narrates his own story in voice-over, explaining how he ended up with those three gunshot wounds. It all began a few months ago.

Racing down Sunset Boulevard from finance men out to repossess his car, Joe has a blow-out and turns into what looks like an abandoned drive-way. He soon finds that the house belongs to silent screen legend Norma Desmond. She welcomes him, thinking he is the undertaker who has come to deliver a coffin for her dead monkey. Joe tells her that he is a screen-writer. Norma is planning a return to the movies and has been writing the script for an epic in which she will play Salome under the direction of C B DeMille. Norma sees in Joe a potential live-in ghost-writer, companion, and lover. Meanwhile, Joe has formed some plans of his own. Ignoring the amateurishness of this odd recluse's script, he senses that he can hustle some easy money to pay off his car by taking Norma's offer for the fix-up job. As he later explains the arrangement, initially it seemed rather recipro-cal: "an older woman who's well-to-do, a younger man who's not doing too well..." On New Year's Eve, however, Joe bristles over his status as a kept man. He and Norma quarrel, and Joe leaves to find some people his own age.

At a party given by his friend Artie Green, Joe re-encounters the normal world. He also again meets Betty Shaefer, Artie's fiancée. Betty is a reader at Paramount who wants to write for the movies. She is familiar with Joe's unproduced scripts and admires their moments of honesty. Joe calls to ask Norma's butler Max to pack his things, and he is shocked to hear that Norma has cut her wrists. Though Joe returns to Norma, seemingly more submissive than ever, he can't get Betty Shaefer out of his mind. A few days later, Max reports a call from Paramount. Norma insists on meeting with DeMille personally. At the studio Max and Joe discover that the calls have come not from DeMille but from a producer wanting to borrow Norma's classic car for a comedy. As Norma prepares for what she thinks is her return to fame, Joe sneaks out at night to write with Betty at Para-mount. With Artie away on location, Joe and Betty begin to fall in love. Norma finds the script pages in Joe's jacket, and she jealously calls Betty to tell her how and with whom Joe lives. By now, Joe wants to trade his success as a gigolo for a chance to reclaim his integrity. He spares Betty nothing about his life with Norma and sends her sadly back to Artie. Joe then packs his suitcase for his return to the copydesk in Dayton, Ohio, leaving the expensive suits and the gold cigarette case. As he walks out the front door, Norma shoots him.

The next morning, Norma has sunk deeper into her delusions. The only way the police can easily get her downstairs is to tell her that the news cameras are really a studio film crew waiting for her to shoot a scene. Max then takes over. Once a director of promise as well as Norma's first husband, Max now directs Norma's descent down the staircase toward her final close-up.

Subtext: A truism of tragedy maintains that the struggles of the hero usually lead to an epiphany, that even though something of value is lost (usually a life), something of value also gets born. *Sunset Boulevard* uses its flashback structure and voice-over narration to exploit this awareness. Joe's comments occur throughout as a kind of ongoing soliloquy.

The film is also a great story of Hollywood rooted in the locations and people of the industry. Brackett and Wilder dot the script with references to real studios, places, and stars. We see DeMille working on the set of *Samson And Delilah*. The natural corollary to this subject becomes the film's emphasis on illusion and the need for a life lie as a coping mechanism. Norma clings to the dream of a return to the ranks of stardom; when Joe finally tells her that the parade's gone by, that it is her devoted Max who writes all the fan letters and safeguards her fragility, he guarantees the tragic outcome. Joe too grapples with the corrosive effects of delayed hope. His self-esteem and essential optimism have shrunk during what has become an extended apprenticeship in Hollywood.

Background: The legendary stature of the film has somewhat obscured its origin. A number of stories exist over who came up with the idea and how it was developed. Years before, Wilder apparently made notes about a project concerning a silent screen star becoming a Hollywood relic. Brackett wanted to develop the premise more comically and had to be won over to the darker aspects of the story. D M Marshman, Jr., one of Wilder's card-playing writer-cronies, reportedly introduced the element of the younger man. Wilder suggested that Norma shoot Joe.

The film boasts one of the most famous rejected scenes in movie history. The original opening scene took place at the morgue where attendants are toe-tagging corpses. The audience sees the bodies on the slabs and hears their voices ask each other how they died. One little boy says that his friend bet him he couldn't stay under water for two minutes: "And I did, too," he says. Preview audiences, however, reacted to this scene with laughter, and Wilder had to introduce Joe's narration and flashback differently. The change was probably a reluctant one since the first draft of the script for his next film, *Ace In The Hole*, began somewhat similarly. (The audience sees the pine box containing the corpse of the protagonist being loaded at a train station. The voice of reporter Kirk Douglas sets up the flashback of his sad fate with language that makes *Ace In The Hole* seem like an expanded newspaper obituary.)

Mae West and Mary Pickford were considered for the part of Norma before George Cukor suggested Swanson to Wilder. Norma screened footage from *Queen Kelly*, an unfinished Swanson picture directed by Erich von Stroheim. Joe's invitation at Paramount to walk Betty back to the office "by way of Washington Square" is a reference to the sets used in *The Heiress*, a William Wyler film shot at Paramount with Montgomery Clift. Cecil B DeMille was offended that his screen credit was originally listed next to that of Franklyn Farnum, the actor playing the man who shows up with the baby casket for the dead chimp. Don Black and Christopher Hampton, who wrote the book for Sir Andrew Lloyd Webber's musical version, retained a surprising amount of dialogue from the film.

Writer David Freeman accompanied Wilder in 1993 to a viewing of the film at Paramount, the first time Wilder had seen *Sunset Boulevard* since its original release. The director's assessment was understated: "There's not too much dust on it... The dialogue was not bad. I didn't wince." Freeman's essay appears in the 21 June 1993 issue of *The New Yorker*. The film won Oscars for best script and music (Franz Waxman) but lost to *All About Eve* in some of its seven other nominated categories.

The Script: The most compelling story screenwriter Joe Gillis ever told is his own. The voice-over narration by a dead man becomes not only a sure-fire hook to capture audience interest but also a vehicle for the tragic insights of a true overreacher. Joe's view from the hereafter is strangely poignant and merciful toward the woman who shot him ("You don't yell at a sleepwalker") and absolutely devoid of self-pity. The clipped tones of Holden's voice suit perfectly the laconic narration. (Brackett and Wilder rewrote portions of the narration after Montgomery Clift backed out of the project.) Joe's rueful self-deprecation also permits audiences to overlook the tawdriness of his scheme to cash in on Norma's desperation.

Wilder's mordant wit has rarely been on better display. When, for example, Norma chooses a day for the big drive to the studio, she consults her astrologer, who reads DeMille's horoscope and then reads Norma's. "Did she read the script?" Joe asks tersely.

The Wilder Mensch: Betty Shaefer, the antithesis of Norma, is the life-affirming force. Betty and Joe fall in love in the most natural way for Wilder characters—while collaborating on a script, their "Untitled Love

Story." This romance blossoms at night as they take a break from the writers' cubby hole at Paramount and tour the deserted, half-built sets. Betty's story about her nose job illustrates the fundamental difference between herself and Joe. She instinctively senses the deceptive nature of the Hollywood system that emphasizes form over substance, and she is happy to forego fame in front of the cameras for what she sees as the greater integrity of writing. Such level-headedness comes harder to Joe, whose appetites are greater and who has to sell out completely in order to realize the same truth. Only after he has bartered his soul does he see the glitter of Hollywood fame and fortune as cheap tinsel.

Meaningful Objects: Is there a single superfluous detail in the film? The swimming pool, for example, becomes the perfect image for Joe. It defines both his susceptibility to the lure of Hollywood status and the ease with which he gets in over his head. It's his bed of comfort and his watery grave. When he climbs out of the pool halfway into the film, he wears swim trunks in the same leopard pattern in which Norma has upholstered her car. It is as if she had stamped him too with her brand. The cars themselves parallel Joe's rise and fall. In California Joe needs wheels to maintain contacts in the picture business; losing the car, he complains, would be like having his legs cut off. But eventually the repo men find his car tucked away in Norma's garage and tow it off. Now his transportation becomes Norma's Isotta-Fraschini, a vehicle as stately and ornate as its owner.

The Visual Element: A number of shots reveal Wilder's career-long skill at finding images that speak as clearly as even the most memorable words. One of these is the stunning shot of Gillis floating dead in the pool photographed from below. Ed Sikov calls this shot, achieved by placing a large mirror on the bottom of the pool, 'spectacularly macabre.' The image of the sound boom ruffling the feather in Norma's outmoded hat encapsulates her obsolescence in the industry in a neat visual shorthand. Other images create the film's distinctive mood: rats in the swimming pool, the wheezing pipe organ, Norma's claw-like cigarette holder. Writer Bernard F Dick puts it well in his book on Wilder when he says that '*Sunset Boulevard* alternates between images of rotting sumptuousness and sumptuous rot.'

The Verdict: Max: "There was a maharajah who came all the way from India to beg one of her silk stockings. Later, he strangled himself with it." Joe: "Well, I sure turned into an interesting driveway." *5/5*

"A Mind Full Of Razor Blades"

William Holden described Wilder with these words, an expression that Wilder later used when referring to the character Walter Matthau plays in *The Fortune Cookie*. After Wilder ended his writing partnership with Charles Brackett, he worked with a number of different collaborators.

Ace In The Hole (1951)
(aka The Big Carnival)

Director: Billy Wilder
Writers: Walter Newman, Lesser Samuels & Billy Wilder
Cast: Kirk Douglas (Chuck Tatum), Jan Sterling (Lorraine), Bob Arthur (Herbie), Porter Hall (Mr Boot), Richard Benedict (Leo Minosa), Ray Teal (Sheriff), 111 minutes

Story: Chuck Tatum has been fired from every big-city newspaper job he has had, all eleven of them. He talks Mr Boot, the editor of the *Albuquerque Sun-Bulletin*, into giving him another chance. A year later Chuck is still mired in New Mexico waiting for the big story that will help him relocate to New York. With Herbie, the young photographer who idolizes him, Chuck drives to Escudero to cover a rattlesnake hunt. He learns there that the owner of the local trading post, Leo Minosa, has been trapped in a cave-in while scrounging for Indian artifacts. Chuck crawls into the burial mound and sees Leo in a blocked-off cavern, his legs pinned under heavy rocks. He interviews Leo and takes his picture. He senses that this is his ticket back to New York.

Chuck orchestrates Leo's story and rescue for maximum publicity. By equating publicity to votes, he entices the local sheriff into authorizing a digging operation that will add days to what should be a sixteen-hour job in reaching Leo. He convinces Lorraine, Leo's cold, bored wife, to stay in Escudero rather than use Leo's entrapment as an excuse to leave him. Once Chuck's newspaper account of the cave-in appears the next day, the morbidly curious descend on Escudero. A circus atmosphere prevails. The cash register at the trading-post and restaurant is full for the first time in years. Lorraine pockets the profits and begins flirting with Chuck.

As the chances of reaching Leo in time diminish, Chuck begins to regret his ruthlessness. He quarrels with and attacks Lorraine, who stabs him with a pair of shears. Mortally injured, Chuck nevertheless brings a priest to the cavern before Leo dies, and he orders the thrill-seekers to disperse. Chuck returns to Mr Boot and collapses dead at his feet.

Subtext: For the second film in a row, Wilder lets his story play out to its tragic ending instead of averting this movement as he did in *The Lost*

51

Weekend. The film scrutinizes the urge to derive entertainment and profit from the misfortune of others; more subtly, it is about people who want out and what they will do to get out. Though Leo is the one literally buried, Lorraine and Chuck also see themselves as buried by forces nearly as stifling.

Background: Walter Newman suggested the premise of the 1925 Floyd Collins cave-in, an event the film refers to. Perhaps because Newman was only twenty years old, Wilder brought in a more experienced hand, Lesser Samuels. At the start of the film, Wilder wanted to replace the Paramount trademark of the star-spangled mountain with a close-up of a hissing rattlesnake. The studio refused. Most critics and movie-goers, however, reacted to the film as if it were a rattlesnake. It was the biggest financial setback of Wilder's career to that point, and as late as 1963 he still referred to it in an interview with *Playboy* magazine as "the runt of the litter." Today, the film seems far ahead of its time. Its attitude toward the press anticipates that of *Network. Mad City,* Costa-Gavras' 1997 film with Dustin Hoffman and John Travolta, is a loose remake of *Ace In The Hole.*

The Script: The dialogue is consistently razor sharp. Wilder credited his wife Audrey with Lorraine's self-defining line, which occurs when she declines to say a rosary for Leo: "I don't go to church. Kneeling bags my nylons." The lyrical montage is a master stroke. Wilder pauses the forward movement of plot in order to savor the human moment of people flocking to gawk at someone else's tragedy. They come by cars and trainloads, and the human carnival has even spawned a ballad that plays on the soundtrack. In this desert setting the high-angle shots of 1200 extras inescapably imply a vulture-like sideshow.

The Wilder Mensch: Why does Mr Boot, the apparent voice of conscience, come across so dully? He is easier to respect than to like, and he is never as compelling as comparable figures in other Wilder films. Boot's defining props are his belt and suspenders, indicative of his over-cautious approach to journalism, and the embroidered sampler 'Tell the Truth' hanging on the newsroom wall. For Boot the search for truth seems to have curdled into platitude. If Herbie is the soul caught between Chuck and the voice of conscience, someone stronger should be pulling on the side of good.

Perhaps Leo himself is the best candidate for this role of conscience. His unassuming goodness and blind trust in Chuck and Lorraine play a bigger part in Chuck's change of heart than the righteous scorn of Mr Boot. Kevin Lally remarks that when Leo receives his last rites, Wilder puts the camera close on Chuck to show that his self-disgust rivals the pain from the lethal stab wound. Ed Sikov interprets this moment as Chuck's own absolution.

Meaningful Objects: Many characters are given a personalizing prop. The crooked sheriff has his pet rattler. Leo's worried mother prays before the votive candles. Lorraine's tawdriness is suggested by the cheap fox fur, which she scorns, just as Leo's touching simplicity emerges in his sureness that she will enjoy this anniversary present.

The Visual Element: A concise transition encompasses Chuck's first year at the paper: he walks toward the camera and blacks out the screen; then he walks away from the camera a year later, still in the same press room, only now he wears both belt and suspenders like Mr Boot. The high shots of Chuck with the drilling crew looking down on the assembled crowd capture the exhilaration of the media circus. The film's final shot delivers a strong impact. Chuck drops dead, landing face first in front of the camera at the feet of Mr Boot.

The Verdict: Pitiless, corrosive, and mean, *Ace In The Hole* is also as honest about Chuck Tatum's eagerness to profit from others' grief as about his profound self-contempt. A tragedy tinged with black comedy (the circus trucks are marked 'The Great S&M Amusement Corp'), the film is an American classic. 5/5

Stalag 17 (1953)

Director: Billy Wilder
Writers: Billy Wilder & Edward Blum, based on the play by Donald Bevan & Edmund Trzcinski
Cast: William Holden (J J Sefton), Don Taylor (Dunbar), Otto Preminger (von Scherbach), Gil Stratton, Jr. (Cookie), Richard Erdman (Hoffy), Robert Strauss (Animal), Harvey Lembeck (Harvey Shapiro), Neville Brand (Duke), Peter Graves (Price), Sig Ruman (Schulz), 120 minutes

Story: The inmates of Barracks Four at the German POW camp Stalag 17 are all sergeants. They have elected their own leader, Hoffy, and security chief, Price. Tonight they send out Manfredi and Johnson through a tunnel in an escape attempt. However, J J Sefton, the barracks profiteer, wonders about the odds. He bets some cigarettes—the currency of exchange among the POWs—against Manfredi and Johnson even making it out of the forest. After a burst of machine-gun fire, Sefton glumly rakes in his winnings—and further alienates himself from the others.

Sefton also trades with the Germans. He keeps an impressive stash in his footlocker, which is inventoried and protected by Cookie, Sefton's only friend. Sefton has added to his hoard by making book on the 'horse races' in the barracks (only he uses mice in a maze), running a distillery from potato mash, and charging two cigarettes a peek through a makeshift telescope pointed at the Russian women's compound. While the rest of the men force down their breakfast swill, Sefton savors an egg he got from the Germans.

A new arrival is Lieutenant Dunbar, whom the sergeants admire for his destruction of a German ammunition train. Hoffy has so far kept the men from turning on Sefton, but when the camp commandant von Scherbach arrests Dunbar for suspicion of sabotage, even Hoffy assumes that Sefton is a traitor working with the Germans. How else can the deaths of Manfredi and Johnson be explained? Or the arrest of Dunbar? One night after lights out, the POWs beat Sefton savagely.

Over the Christmas holiday, Sefton nurses his wounds and warily observes his barrack mates. He finally discovers during an air-raid blackout the identity of the German spy. He weighs his options and implements his own plan on the day the POWs attempt to free Dunbar from the Germans. Later, with Dunbar in hiding on the grounds, Sefton exposes the informer. Sefton then volunteers to round up Dunbar and escort him past the barbed wire to safety. The Americans now have the spy to throw into the compound before the watchtower guards as a diversion. For the first time, Sefton likes the odds.

Subtext: The real strength of the film is Sefton. The premise must have held irresistible appeal to the iconoclastic Wilder. The good American patriots all descend to vigilantism, beating their fellow POW to a pulp and stealing from his footlocker, while the non-conformist Sefton uses his ostracism to expose the German spy. The keepers of the barracks status quo then become so concerned with punishing the spy that they hardly express any regrets for their treatment of Sefton. Few films show as clearly the perils and sheer stupidity of mindless conformity. Not surprisingly, it was made during the era of the McCarthy witch hunts and the Hollywood blacklist.

Background: Wilder needed a big hit to bounce back from the disappointing response to *Ace In The Hole.* He chose the safety of a popular Broadway play, and the film became a success. CNN interviewer Larry King recently asked Kirk Douglas if there was a particular part he had turned down that he later regretted. Douglas named the role of Sefton. He said that he had seen the play on which the film was to be based and was unimpressed. Curiously, Holden too had seen the play and walked out after the first act. According to Wilder biographer Kevin Lally, the director encouraged Holden to wait until he read the script before rejecting the project. (Charlton Heston had also been briefly considered but evidently not offered the part.) Holden, who became very close to Wilder over the years, enjoyed needling his friend by pointing out that he was not Wilder's first choice in either *Sunset Boulevard* or *Stalag 17*, their two most famous collaborations.

The Script: Wilder and co-writer Edward Blum coarsened Sefton's character to make him more of an outsider and to sharpen the rift in the barracks. The internal feud between the POWs and Sefton adds a dramatic edge and prevents any easy sentimentality from falsifying the film. Some of the actors from the Broadway play (Robert Strauss, Harvey Lembeck) were recruited for the movie.

The Wilder Mensch: Everyone turns on Sefton, even Cookie. Leaving the voice of conscience out of this film intensifies the starkness of the prison-camp atmosphere.

Meaningful Objects: Sefton's 'department store' (i.e., his footlocker full of loot) reveals both his profiteering impulse and his status as a loner. A hollowed-out chess piece becomes the mailbox for the German informer to communicate with the guard. A mistaken shipment of ping pong balls later figures importantly as a tool in the rescue of Dunbar. The plaintive sounds from Crazy Joey's ocarina become a musical lament of prison-camp life.

Von Scherbach's boots are used to reveal his hopes for advancement. When, for example, he interrogates Dunbar, von Scherbach paces across his office in his socks. Preparing to receive a call from Berlin, however, he has his assistant help him on with his boots, and then stands at attention clicking his heels while on the phone with the Third Reich. After the call, he removes his boots and again in his socks disdainfully welcomes the inspector from the Geneva Convention.

The Visual Element: The second hour of the film, thanks to some impressive editing and camera moves, adds subtlety and subtext to what begins as a rather straightforward story. No other Wilder film affords such a clear separation between verbal and visual strengths. In the first half, the camera functions essentially as a recording apparatus. Wilder often de-emphasizes editing and films the prisoners in tightly-framed scenes crowded with faces in foreground, midground, and background. Such shots unfold like little one-act plays and work because the strong writing establishes setting and character.

After Sefton is beaten up by his fellow prisoners, editing and camera movement become more prominent. Sefton and the audience, for example, discover the identity of the spy in a pictorial way. The shadow of the swinging light bulb alerts Sefton to the signal (a knot in the cord) used by the spy to communicate with the Germans. After Sefton has verified the identity of the informer, Wilder capitalizes on the knowledge the audience shares with Sefton to create some powerful scenes. In one striking pair of matched shots, the camera slowly tracks from the spy in the foreground through prisoners dancing and decorating the barracks for Christmas to a close-up of Sefton sitting reflectively on his bunk. The next shot reverses this pattern, starting from Sefton's point of view and slowly tracking through the dancing men to a close-up of the spy in his false security. Wordlessly, these shots intensify audience identification with Sefton and underscore the cat-and-mouse game in which Sefton ponders how to use his knowledge of the culprit.

Another great example of the omniscient camera is the impressive high-angle long shot of the 600 prisoners called into the compound as the Germans search for the escaped Dunbar. Von Scherbach, increasingly angry and baffled, knows that Dunbar is still in the camp somewhere. The camera pans discreetly to the right, revealing the water tower over the south latrine and, just visible inside the tank, a crouching Dunbar, wrapped around a ladder to stay above the water.

A famous remark by François Truffaut maintains that "movies in which characters lie require more shots than movies in which characters tell the truth." The second half of *Stalag 17* provides a great example. One of Wilder's least recognized gifts as a director is his versatility at using such different, accomplished styles to serve his material. The first half of *Stalag 17*, therefore, resembles the austerity of a William Wyler film while the second half is pure Hitchcock. It's an effective combination.

The Verdict: Though some of the comedy grows tiresome, especially the antics of the camp impressionist, the ensemble works well, and William Holden delivers one of his most memorable performances. 4/5

Sabrina (1954)
(aka Sabrina Fair)

Director: Billy Wilder
Writers: Billy Wilder, Ernest Lehman & Samuel Taylor, based on Taylor's play *Sabrina Fair*
Cast: Humphrey Bogart (Linus Larrabee), Audrey Hepburn (Sabrina Fairchild), William Holden (David Larrabee), John Williams (Fairchild), Walter Hampden (Oliver Larrabee), Marcel Dalio (The Baron), Francis X Bushman (Mr Tyson), Ellen Corby (Miss McCardle), 113 minutes

Story: On the night before she leaves for a two-year cooking course in Paris, Sabrina Fairchild, the chauffeur's daughter at the palatial Long Island estate of the Larrabees, watches the family's younger son, David, make yet another romantic conquest. Sabrina has had a crush on David since they were children; her father hopes that two years in Paris will remedy that. When Sabrina returns from Paris transformed, David can't believe that the gawky tomboy he used to roller skate with is now a beautiful, sophisticated woman. David pursues Sabrina, but Linus, the older Larrabee brother, fears that his promised plastics merger will fall through. Linus intends for David to marry the daughter of a sugar cane tycoon so that Larrabee Industries can manufacture a new plastic that is both durable and sweet tasting.

Linus plots to break up David and Sabrina. Noticing that David has hidden two champagne glasses in his back pockets for his later rendezvous with Sabrina, Linus asks David to sit down. Later, with his brother painfully recuperating from stitches in his behind, Linus romances Sabrina, even though he seems to be already married to his job. Both Sabrina and Linus are surprised by their mutual affection. They end up on an ocean liner to Paris while David happily goes through with the marriage and the merger.

Subtext: A romance and comedy across social classes emphasizes the need for transformation and the rejuvenating power of love.

Background: Samuel Taylor quit the collaboration when he saw the radical changes Wilder intended for his play. The strict shooting schedules of the three stars necessitated some hectic work by Wilder and Ernest Lehman, who replaced Taylor. The famous ordeal of making this film might serve as the basis for an interesting film itself. The crankiness of Bogart and the resulting friction between director and star (later resolved) as well as the writing sessions of Wilder and Lehman have become Hollywood legend.

Sydney Pollack screened his remake for Wilder in 1995. *USA Today* recorded Wilder's reaction to the nervous Pollack when the lights came up: "Sydney, how would you like it if I remade *The Way We Were*?"

The Script: The opening scene makes about as perfect a beginning as any romantic comedy ever had. The image of Audrey Hepburn as the tomboy observing the elegant party from a tree and averting her eyes at David's flirtations with another woman initiates the romantic conflict in an indelibly visual way. It is remarkable that such a classic script could have been turned out under such tense conditions.

The Wilder Mensch: Paris is virtually a character in the film, and it is the spirit of 'La Vie en Rose' that transforms, first Sabrina, then Linus. "Paris is not for changing planes," she instructs Linus, the cold corporate executive. "It's for changing your outlook." Butte, Montana, the dreaded location of Larrabee Copper, becomes a sort of anti-Paris, the spot of exile that

David wants to avoid at all costs. The conservatism of Sabrina's loving father partially prevents him from taking over this role of the life-affirming force. "Don't reach for the moon, child," he cautions Sabrina. When Fairchild explains his class philosophy that life is like the limousine he drives ("with a front seat, a back seat, and a window in between"), Linus jokingly calls him a snob.

Meaningful Objects: Goldfish humanize Sabrina. She knows the name of George, the pet goldfish in the Larrabee fountain, and she stops to feed her own fish, tapping the glass to make sure they eat, before she goes off for her melodramatic suicide attempt. This little action reminds us that we're in the world of comedy and that of course she won't succeed at killing herself.

Linus' depersonalizing attention to work is suggested by the buttons and gadgets in his office as well as by his umbrella and homburg (which Sabrina repeatedly adjusts to make more becoming). Kevin Lally wrote that Cary Grant turned down the role because he didn't like the idea of having to carry the umbrella. David's shallowness shows in his straw hat, his roadster, and the hammock with the hole in it. His scarred backside, however, becomes the defining image for this silly playboy. Old man Larrabee's all-thumbs approach to life is revealed in the running joke of his inability to extract an olive from a jar. The rigidity of the entire Larrabee family, in fact, is conveyed by their poses in the family portrait over the mantle, the same stances they assume in the opening scene. Is this the family's only moment of togetherness—assembling for the annual photograph at the party to celebrate the six-meter yacht race?

The Visual Element: The same wit that turns up in the dialogue also appears in the visual exaggeration and cleverness of the *mise en scène*. Sabrina's suicide attempt, for example, takes place inside the Larrabee garage with a comic perspective of eight idling limousines and one jalopy blowing smoke rings out its exhaust. Linus tests the strength of his new plastic by calling in a squadron of matronly secretaries to bounce on it with an embarrassed David; later, he repeats the trick with tuxedoed party guests. When Linus leaves his last board meeting, he trots through a receding series of doors in his farewell to the cavernous, lonely life of the business executive.

The Verdict: A few bumps appear in the cinematic road—the cooking school scenes could do with some more life; Hepburn creates more chemistry with Holden than with Bogart—but Wilder chauffeurs the audience along smoothly in an exceptionally memorable film. *4/5*

The Seven Year Itch (1955)

Director: Billy Wilder
Writers: Billy Wilder & George Axelrod, based on Axelrod's play
Cast: Marilyn Monroe (the girl), Tom Ewell (Richard Sherman), Evelyn Keyes (Helen Sherman), Sonny Tufts (Tom McKenzie), Robert Strauss (Kruhulik), Oscar Homolka (Dr Brubaker), 105 minutes

Story: As soon as Richard Sherman, a book editor, sends off his wife and son to Maine for the summer, he instinctively ogles a passing girl at the train station. "Oh, no, not me," he cautions himself, "and I'm not going to smoke, either." But his eyes persist in wandering. The manuscript he is currently reading defines 'the seven year itch and the urge curve' as the desire of middle-aged husbands and summer bachelors like Richard to cheat on their wives. More pressure comes from the beautiful young actress who has sublet the upstairs apartment for the summer. In the sweltering New York heat, Richard tells himself that he is only being neighborly by inviting the girl down for a drink. His air-conditioning makes them comfortably chatty. Over the next two days, this would-be playboy wrestles with his conscience, torn between the pictures of fulfillment and exposure that his wild imagination conjures up for him.

Eventually, the girl does some planning herself. A television model, she has an early call at the studio, and to be fresh for work she seems rather willing, if necessary, to swap some lovemaking for a cool bed for the night. After the girl opens the interior staircase connecting their apartments—she pulls out the nails in the trapdoor over the stairs and descends like a goddess from above—Richard offers her a bed, but he gallantly sleeps on the sofa. She now sees beyond his ordinariness to his gentle nature. The next morning she kisses him and tells him that his wife is wrong not to be jealous of him. On an impulse, Richard offers the girl his air-conditioned apartment and runs off to spend an impromptu vacation with his wife and son.

Subtext: The entire film is essentially an elaboration of the first scene from *The Major And The Minor*. That film opens with Robert Benchley as a restless husband whose wife and son are away. His timid philandering takes the form of ordering scalp massages and hoping that the woman who shows up at his door will be both attractive and receptive. The comic suspense of these two uncertainties and the thrill of doing something naughty provide his gratification. *The Seven Year Itch* gives its husband, Richard Sherman, a trace of a conscience along with the imagination of a Walter Mitty, but the picture remains primarily a skit stretched out to feature-length proportions.

Background: This was Wilder's first film after he ended his association with Paramount. Wilder told Professor Richard Brown in a 1993 interview for the US Library of Congress that he wanted to add a short scene in which a maid finds a hairpin in Richard's bed, an indication that he and the girl slept together. But Twentieth-Century Fox was already nervous about the adulterous implications of the film and didn't want more problems. The references in the script to the girl's beach photo printed in *US Camera* imply that it was a nude picture. When Richard shows the photo to Dr Brubaker in his office, however, the studio has added a cutaway to Marilyn in a swimsuit to sanitize things even more. Walter Matthau did a screen test for the lead, but Tom Ewell got the part since his was the more familiar and bankable name.

The Script: Some of the satire—of book publishers putting lurid covers on classic novels, of the beach scene in *From Here To Eternity*, of psychotherapy—has dated the film. The opening narration is probably less subtle than that in any other Wilder film, and the script has fewer memorable lines than most by Wilder.

The Wilder Mensch: Sherman's conscience, feeble though it is, troubles him just enough to create some comic tension but not enough to sustain the film. His comic hesitations about adultery are really his way of auditioning the idea. They mostly involve a fear of what others, like the building superintendent, might think. The ease with which Richard switches from lust to remorse humanizes him; his middle-class, moral pettiness becomes both his chief flaw and his saving grace. Richard's boss, Mr Brady, on the other hand, is presented as a husband who has happily killed off his conscience long ago. Having sent away his wife for the summer, Brady spends the night playing poker and tells Richard he hopes to get lucky in other ways, too. He represents what Richard is in danger of becoming.

Meaningful Objects: The sealed-off staircase to the girl's apartment upstairs serves as a visual reminder both of Richard's desires and of his difficulty in achieving them. The canoe paddle that Richard's son forgets and that Richard seems constantly to carry is integrated smoothly into the plot. A reminder of his role as a father, its exaggerated phallic shape also suggests his futile efforts at concealing his frustrated longings.

The Visual Element: The visuals disappoint perhaps because it was Wilder's first CinemaScope film. He would use widescreen compositions much more effectively in *The Spirit Of St Louis* and *The Apartment*. The famous picture of Marilyn with her billowing dress was removed from the film itself and used as a publicity shot, evidently for censorship reasons. In the film, when she stands over the subway grating and the passing train makes her dress billow, we never see her in a full shot.

The Verdict: Marilyn's performance gives the girl an irresistible blend of sweetness and sexual practicality. The distinctive stamp on this film is more Monroe's than Wilder's. *2/5*

The Spirit Of St Louis (1957)

Director: Billy Wilder
Writers: Billy Wilder, Wendell Mayes & Charles Lederer, based on the book by Charles Lindbergh
Cast: James Stewart (Charles Lindbergh), Murray Hamilton (Bud Gurney), Marc Connelly (Father Hussman), Patricia Smith (Girl with the mirror), 135 minutes

Story: Charles Lindbergh is too nervous to sleep the night before his transatlantic flight in 1927. He remembers his meeting with the group of St Louis investors who have agreed to sponsor him. He recalls overseeing the construction of his plane in San Diego. After a dangerous take-off the next morning at Roosevelt Field, Lindbergh occupies the 33 hours of his flight with reveries about his first plane, his barnstorming days, and his stint in the army. He battles against ice on his wings and the need for sleep. Finally safe in Paris, the exhausted aviator is greeted as a hero.

Subtext: A laudatory look at self-determination. The opening titles suggest that the film also intends to offer an inside glimpse at history in the making.

Background: Producer Leland Hayward purchased the film rights to Lindbergh's 1953 biography and brought in Wilder to write and direct. Wilder felt that he never really got to know the real Lindbergh and consequently struggled with the character. It is Wilder's least personal film and was a failure at the box office.

The Script: The second hour suffers from too much voice-over narration. The points about Lindbergh's fear of ice on the wings and his confusion in locating Ireland could probably be made more subtly and dramatically through editing (in the manner used to suggest Don Birnam's thirst during the opera scene in *The Lost Weekend*).

The Wilder Mensch: A priest's St Christopher medal is dropped into Lindbergh's lunch sack by a friend minutes before take-off. The editing of his approach to foggy Le Bourget field suggests that God has brought in the agnostic pilot safely.

Meaningful Objects: Wilder uses a number of props to add human interest to a story whose outcome is well known to the audience. A young woman gives Lindbergh a pocket mirror for his dashboard so that he can see the compass mounted over his head. (The sun's reflection in the mirror later wakes him when he dozes off during the flight.) The personable owner of the aviation plant in San Diego cooks sand dabs in the factory with a blow torch on a sheet of aluminum. Lindbergh's pals back at Lambert Field in St Louis chart his course by drawing a line from a map of the US across a wall to a knot-hole that represents Paris.

The Visual Element: In his only attempt to make an epic (not counting the truncated *Sherlock Holmes*), Wilder directed a film that is impressive in all respects except character. One might expect the opposite from a director who prided himself on his writing and who rarely worked in color. The conundrum posed by the stoical Charles Lindbergh simply eluded him. Nevertheless, the location footage is beautiful, the camera seems always in the perfect place, and the montages of Lindbergh's take-off and landing are virtuoso set pieces without a single wasted shot.

The Verdict: The photography, music (by Franz Waxman), and epic sweep are all impressive, but the film never overcomes the lifelessness of looking at Lindbergh from the outside rather than the inside. *3/5*

"Why Not?"

I A L Diamond became Wilder's collaborator during his later years. Wilder said that the two friends would go to the office like the employees of a bank. The highest accolade one could receive from the stoical Diamond, Wilder said, was the comment, "Why not?"

Love In The Afternoon (1957)

Director: Billy Wilder
Writers: Billy Wilder & I A L Diamond, based on the novel *Ariane* by Claude Anet
Cast: Gary Cooper (Frank Flannagan), Audrey Hepburn (Ariane Chevasse), Maurice Chevalier (Claude Chevasse), John McGiver (Mr X), Van Doude (Michel), 125 minutes

Story: Parisian detective Claude Chevasse has tried in vain to keep his pretty young daughter Ariane from reading his files. Most of his recent work has involved tracing the amorous adventures of Frank Flannagan, an American millionaire seemingly irresistible to married women. Ariane eavesdrops on her father's report to a husband cuckolded by the charming Flannagan. This one vows to shoot him.

Ariane rushes to Flannagan's rescue. Sneaking into his hotel suite at the Ritz, Ariane warns Flannagan minutes before the angry husband confronts them; Ariane pretends to be Flannagan's companion. She later playfully refuses to tell a grateful Flannagan who she is. He is as intrigued by her innocent mystery as she is by the mystery of his experience. She returns to him the next afternoon, and they both agree that love without entanglements is the most satisfying. On Flannagan's next trip to Paris, he sees Ariane at the opera, and their romance develops. Using lurid events culled from her father's cases, she itemizes her 'lovers' on Flannagan's Dictaphone, ranging from a red-headed algebra teacher to a Dutch alcoholic. Flannagan, now fascinated and jealous, must know who she is. In a Turkish bath, he meets up again with the cuckolded husband, who recommends the services of Claude Chevasse. Flannagan reports the girl's colorful history to the detective, who recognizes the fragments of his own cases. Chevasse tells Flannagan that the girl is his daughter and that she is in love. The worried father cautions Flannagan that she is just a "little fish" and asks him to throw her back. Flannagan decides to leave Paris. Ariane accompanies him to the train station, tearfully insisting on love without entanglements. Flannagan, however, cannot leave her. He sweeps her up into the train with him, his cynical reserve now lovingly entangled by her charm and innocence.

Subtext: The film concerns a rake's regress, or as Chevasse explains it, the irony of the "hit-and-run lover" who gets run over himself.

Background: The film is Wilder's affectionate tribute to the cinema of Ernst Lubitsch. It is closer in tone to the high sophistication and refinement of Lubitsch's masterpiece *Trouble In Paradise* than the more romantic *Ninotchka*. Wilder described to Cameron Crowe his unsuccessful attempts to find a vehicle for Cary Grant, who was sought for the leads in *Ninotchka, Five Graves To Cairo, Sabrina* (the Bogart role), and this film. Somehow, Wilder explained, Grant always "slipped through the net." Wilder's wife Audrey appears as Flannagan's date at the opera.

The Script: As beautifully assembled as a Swiss watch, the script features one of the most satisfying third acts of Wilder's career. The ironic inevitability of the lovesick Flannagan getting advice from the husband he has cuckolded is richly satisfying. The subsequent resolution plays out with a perfect balance of emotion and logic.

The Wilder Mensch: Claude Chevasse, the caring, protective father, shows his love for his only daughter by investigating her boyfriend Michel. As he delightfully explains it, "If I were an Indian potentate, I would shower you with diamonds. If I were a cobbler, I would sole your shoes. But since I am detective, I can only offer you a detailed dossier." Ariane beams in loving appreciation.

Meaningful Objects: The film is one of Wilder's richest at using objects to reveal character and to advance the plot. The contrast between Ariane's mundane reality and her romantic fictions is suggested by the incongruity of her cello case and the ermine coat she borrows (as well as by the chain on the case that she transforms into an anklet when meeting Flannagan). His lapel carnation (which she takes as a keepsake), four-piece Gypsy band (which even accompanies him to the Turkish bath), and their signature song 'Fascination' illustrate his stylish decadence. Flannagan replays Ariane's list of lovers over and over on the Dictaphone, a sign of his growing obsession with her.

The Visual Element: Wilder indulges his love of mirror shots with an appropriately poetic image. Ariane stands on the balcony next to a French door, and we see reflected in the glass the shrouded image of the mysterious Flannagan. Their dialogue plays with no cutting. In the nooks and crannies of Chevasse's office/apartment and Flannagan's spacious hotel suite, deep-space shots take full advantage of art director Alexander Trauner's beautiful designs. Editing, however, also discloses character and adds wit. When Ariane seems to be practicing her cello, for example, she really has Flannagan's file open on her music stand. The cutting alternates shots of her wide-eyed wonder, the scandalous clippings, and her father's frowns at her numerous sour notes.

The Verdict: Probably few would prefer the somewhat haggard Cooper over ageless Cary Grant, but the film is written, directed, and performed with consummate charm and finesse. *4/5*

Witness For The Prosecution (1957)

Director: Billy Wilder
Writers: Billy Wilder & Harry Kurnitz, adaptation by Larry Marcus, based on the play by Agatha Christie
Cast: Tyrone Power (Leonard Vole), Charles Laughton (Sir Wilfrid Robarts), Marlene Dietrich (Christine Vole), Elsa Lanchester (Miss Plimsoll), John Williams (Brogan-Moore), Henry Daniell (Mayhew), Ian Wolfe (Carter), Una O'Connor (Janet McKenzie), Norma Varden (Mrs French), Ruta Lee (Diana), 116 minutes

Story: Barrister Sir Wilfrid Robarts is convinced of the innocence of murder suspect Leonard Vole in spite of strong circumstantial evidence. Vole, a struggling inventor, cultivated a friendship with Mrs French, a wealthy widow flattered by the attentions of a younger man. Vole seems to have presented himself to Mrs French as a bachelor even though he is married to Christine, a German refugee. Vole admits that on the night of Mrs French's murder he visited her, but he insists on his innocence. When he inherits a sizable portion of her estate, the police arrest him.

Christine holds his only alibi. Sir Wilfrid is dismayed to discover that Christine is not legally married to Vole and took part in a ceremony with him only to escape post-war Berlin. Christine becomes the surprise witness for the prosecution, and in open court she reverses her story of Vole's innocence. Back in his chambers, Sir Wilfrid despairs over the case when a phone call from a mysterious woman changes everything. She sells Sir Wilfrid a packet of letters written by Christine to a secret lover. In them, Christine promises to lie in court about Vole's guilt so that she can be free of him. Sir Wilfrid uses the letters to break Christine down on the witness stand, but that is only the first of many twists in a surprising conclusion.

Subtext: The whodunit structure introduces the theme of deception and disguise, two ideas that recur throughout Wilder's work.

Background: Producer Edward Small purchased the screen rights to Agatha Christie's 1953 play that had run for 458 performances in London and 644 in New York. The exact development of the movie project is a bit unclear. Director Joshua Logan seems to have advised Small and producer Arthur Hornblow on the casting, or perhaps Logan was the first one offered the job of directing, as some sources indicate. Why Wilder did not collaborate with I A L Diamond after their work on *Love In The Afternoon* also seems a bit vague. Harry Kurnitz had published some murder mysteries under the pseudonym Marco Page, so perhaps that gave him sufficient standing to undertake an Agatha Christie rewrite with Wilder.

The Script: Like her novels, Christie's play is brilliant in its plotting but thin on character. Wilder and Kurnitz slightly changed the play's emphasis from Vole to Sir Wilfrid. They infuse nearly all the characters with fuller personalities, especially Sir Wilfrid. In the opening scene, he returns to his office from a hospital convalescence following a heart attack. In his typically gruff way, he accepts the well-wishes of his little family of office workers. He also directs a running barrage of insults at Miss Plimsoll (played by Laughton's wife, Elsa Lanchester), a frighteningly cheerful nurse who is not in Christie's play at all. Her recuperative mission is to keep Sir Wilfrid from cases that might overly excite him, like the one brought by Leonard Vole. The two flashbacks and some of Sir Wilfrid's courtroom tricks (such as hiding the packet of letters when questioning Christine) are also Wilder contributions. Even in scenes that follow Christie closely in plot, the dialogue of the play is extensively rewritten and sharpened. For example, after Vole says that he met Mrs French when she was buying a hat, Sir Wilfrid sardonically adds, "I'm constantly surprised that women's hats don't provoke more murders."

The Wilder Mensch: Miss Plimsoll is one of the best comic illustrations of this life-affirming force in the entire Wilder canon. Her comments from the gallery during the trial parallel the reactions of the audience. After the surprises of the ending, she encourages Sir Wilfrid once again to come to the defense of a needy victim, and she and Sir Wilfrid leave the Old Bailey arm in arm.

Meaningful Objects: Sir Wilfrid administers 'the monocle test' to both Vole and Christine on different occasions as he questions them in his office. Suggesting the incisiveness of Sir Wilfrid's quick mind, it is his typically flamboyant way of verifying the truthfulness of a client. Sir Wilfrid reflects the sunlight with his monocle onto their faces like the light of an interrogation lamp. Vole passively sits and withstands its glare; Christine strides to the window and pulls down the shade.

The Visual Element: As with many screen adaptations of plays, scenes often unfold with minimal cutting and with characters positioned within the frame to emphasize deep space. The scenes in Sir Wilfrid's office are good examples of this unobtrusive directorial style.

The Verdict: Delightful if unambitious. 4/5

Some Like It Hot (1959)

Director: Billy Wilder
Writers: Billy Wilder & I A L Diamond, based on a screen story by Robert Thoeren & M Logan
Cast: Marilyn Monroe (Sugar Kane), Tony Curtis (Joe), Jack Lemmon (Jerry), George Raft (Spats Columbo), Pat O'Brien (Mulligan), Joe E Brown (Osgood Fielding), 120 minutes

Story: In Prohibition Chicago, Joe and Jerry witness the St Valentine's Day Massacre and barely escape a spray of machine-gun bullets from Spats Columbo. With all of gangland Chicago looking for them, they disguise themselves as girls and join an all-girl band traveling to Miami. Joe, dressed as Josephine, cautions Jerry, who is now Daphne, not to blow their cover: "Just keep telling yourself you're a girl." Late at night during a party on the train to Miami, however, Joe finds it hard to follow his own advice when Sugar, the vocalist with the band, reveals her romantic disappointments.

In Miami, Joe disguises himself as Junior, an oil millionaire, to continue his flirtation with Sugar. He instructs Jerry to accept a date with Osgood Fielding, the much-married older man who pinched Daphne in the elevator, so that he, as Junior, can romance Sugar on Osgood's yacht. That night Joe pretends impotence so that Sugar will undertake some charity work (she once sold kisses for the Milk Fund) in trying to arouse him. On shore, Osgood and Jerry (as Daphne) dance until dawn. The next morning the Milk Fund is richer and a giddy Jerry has accepted Osgood's wedding proposal. Joe now reverses his advice: "Just keep telling yourself you're a boy."

Spats Columbo and his hoods arrive in Miami and soon recognize Josephine and Daphne as the two musicians from the Chicago garage. Before fleeing from Spats, Joe lingers as Josephine to try to ease Sugar's disappointment over Junior's rejection. Sugar follows Joe and Jerry to the pier where Osgood waits in a motor boat. Joe and Sugar reconcile, and Jerry takes off his wig as Daphne and tells Osgood that he can't marry him because he's a man. Osgood shrugs and smiles: "Well, nobody's perfect."

Subtext: A farcical comedy of identity blends with a satire of gangster movies. Joe's disguise eventually emphasizes romantic comedy while Jerry's satirizes the supposedly clear distinctions of gender. Sugar presents herself to Junior as one of the social elite to catch the millionaire, and even the hoods pretend to be 'The Friends of Italian Opera' for their murderous convention in Miami. Leland A Poague phrases it well when he writes that 'every character in *Some Like It Hot* is searching for the right costume, the right style.'

Background: The only useful idea, evidently, that came from the source material was the musicians-as-girls premise. Everything else—Prohibition Chicago, gangsters, Miami, millionaires, hot jazz—came from Wilder and Diamond. Frank Sinatra was originally considered for one of the male leads. The legendary difficulties of multiple retakes posed by a distraught Monroe aggravated her relationships with Wilder and Curtis. Watching the daily rushes of the yacht scenes, Curtis let slip the now-famous barb that it was like "kissing Hitler."

The Script: The transgender humor of Joe and Jerry in drag is so effective that it becomes easy to overlook the other comic elements of the script. George Meredith's famous remark that true comedy evokes "thoughtful laughter" applies to *Some Like It Hot.* The film is as rich in the comedy of human nature as in the sure-fire premises of situational humor. Wilder and Diamond constantly exploit the audience's full awareness of who is who under the disguises. For example, when Sugar tells Josephine that she has a weakness for tenor sax players, the audience enjoys the moment because they can correctly see in Josephine's interested reaction Joe's own libido kicking in. Later, on the beach Sugar's story of her privileged past is made up partly from details she's picked up from Josephine and Daphne on the train. The running joke about type-O blood is not so much a funny punch line as a way of inviting the audience to identify further with Joe and Jerry. Joe first reports that he and Jerry have the same type blood in the office of the booking agent. He later uses the joke to remind Jerry of the need to stay ahead of Spats and the hoods: "I see blood everywhere—type O." Blood also figures in Joe's story to Sugar of Junior's impotence (his transfusions failed to revive his beloved who fell into the Grand Canyon). The script thus depends on insider knowledge of both its characters and of events. When at the outset Joe tells Jerry not to be so negative, he mentions some seemingly unthinkable 'what ifs' for the 1920s, all of which of course later occurred: the divorce of Mary Pickford and Douglas Fairbanks, the crash of the stock market, the departure of the Brooklyn Dodgers for Los Angeles.

The Wilder Mensch: Josephine humanizes Joe or, more accurately, Josephine gets to know Sugar and hear of her vulnerabilities, which humanizes Sugar in Joe's eyes and makes him want to treat her better. Joe gives Sugar the valuable bracelet that Osgood gave Daphne, even though it is the only thing Joe and Jerry have to live on once they leave the girls' band. Joe also interrupts the final escape when he hears Sugar's mournful rendition of 'I'm Through With Love' on the bandstand. Dressed as Josephine, he rushes up to her and kisses her passionately—an amazing moment—and

68

comforts her: "None of that, Sugar. No guy's worth it." Sugar mentally puts Junior and Josephine together and rushes off to catch up with Joe.

Meaningful Objects: Spats' gangland superiority is suggested by his flashy footwear, just as Toothpick Charlie's low-life status is defined by the toothpick Spats rudely kicks out of his mouth after rubbing him out. The double bass becomes a comic prop as Jerry lugs it around when he and Joe are on the run. "Look at the bull fiddle," Jerry says after Joe has hocked their overcoats for a losing dogtrack bet: "It's dressed warmer than I am." The band manager's round horn-rims and clothing provide Joe with his identity as Junior. (The Cary Grant imitation was Tony Curtis' idea when Wilder asked him for an accent to personalize the character.) Sugar's flask reflects her despair over being unlucky in love: "It's the story of my life—I always get the fuzzy end of the lollipop."

The Visual Element: Diamond contributed the idea of making the film a period piece. When everyone is wearing costumes, he reasoned, two guys in drag will seem less outlandish. The decision to shoot in black-and-white came about for the same reason. The garishness of the make-up would be less prominent, and the historical flavor would come across more effectively.

The Verdict: The film placed first in the recent survey by the American Film Institute of top screen comedies. *5/5*

The Apartment (1960)

Director: Billy Wilder
Writers: Billy Wilder & I A L Diamond
Cast: Jack Lemmon (C C Bud Baxter), Shirley MacLaine (Fran Kubelik), Fred MacMurray (J D Sheldrake), Ray Walston (Dobisch), David Lewis (Kirkeby), Jack Kruschen (Dr Dreyfuss), 125 minutes

Story: Bud Baxter works at desk 861 at Consolidated Life Insurance. He has been lending his apartment key alternately to four philandering executives who want a place to take their girlfriends. Called to the office of personnel director J D Sheldrake, Bud gladly accepts the well-wishes of Fran Kubelik, the elevator girl he has a crush on. Bud expects a promotion thanks to glowing efficiency reports from his four friends. Instead, Sheldrake surprises Bud by confronting him with his knowledge of the floating apartment key. Bud seems relieved. Unable to say no to people, Bud has exhausted himself in trying to please the four insatiable executives. Sheldrake surprises Bud again by asking to use Bud's apartment himself or rather to swap two theater tickets for use of the key. Bud invites Fran to the theater, but, unknown to Bud, Fran is the woman Sheldrake plans to take that night to Bud's apartment. Earlier, Fran had ended their affair when Sheldrake wouldn't leave his wife. Now, she stands Bud up for their date at the theater when Sheldrake tells her that he is ready for a divorce.

Weeks pass. Bud gets his promotion, and Sheldrake continues to take Fran to the apartment. At the office Christmas party, Bud discovers that Fran is Sheldrake's mistress and Fran learns that Sheldrake has strung along many women with the same lie about divorcing his wife. At the apartment, however, Sheldrake seems unperturbed when Fran confronts him. After he leaves, Fran attempts suicide by swallowing sleeping pills. Bud returns home to find her nearly dead. He and his neighbor, Dr Drey-fuss, manage to save her life. Over Christmas, a lovesick Bud nurses Fran with conversation, gin rummy games, and a home-made Italian dinner. He also tries unsuccessfully to get Sheldrake to show some concern.

Things change, however, when Sheldrake's wife decides to divorce him after hearing of his infidelities. Sheldrake tells Bud, whose office now adjoins his own, that he looks forward to the life of a bachelor, though he has Fran penciled in as the next Mrs Sheldrake. Bud abruptly quits. On New Year's Eve with Fran, Sheldrake reports the sudden resignation of this "little punk" and Bud's sudden refusal to let him take Fran to the apartment. Fran leaves Sheldrake and rushes back to the apartment to find Bud.

Subtext: The film teems with edgy, fresh ideas: that conformity in the American workplace saps (and ultimately sells out) the soul, that our actions in conforming probably result more from the selfishness and hunger for advancement than (as we would like to think) from the insecurity of not fitting in, and that the necessary ingredient to break such a debilitating cycle is not self-knowledge (as we would think) but decent and compassionate treatment from others.

This last point is wonderfully illustrated by Fran. She tells Bud as he cooks their dinner that Sheldrake is "a taker. Some people take; some people get took. And they know they're getting took and there's nothing they can do about it." If self-knowledge were sufficiently empowering, Fran's clear awareness of her self-victimization should assist her. But she still foolishly yearns for Sheldrake's love. It is only when she hears that Bud has refused to let Sheldrake take Fran to the apartment—only when another person has treated her decently—that she takes action. Wilder italicizes this moment with a long close-up of Fran in the booth at the Chinese restaurant putting it all together and making the realization of a lifetime.

Background: Wilder said he was intrigued by the unseen character in David Lean's *Brief Encounter*, the guy who lent the lovers his apartment and later had to crawl back himself into that warm bed. Out of that premise

70

grew *The Apartment*. The film was the basis for the Broadway musical *Promises, Promises*, which ran for 1,281 performances from 1968 to 1972. Wilder took home three Oscars for his work producing, directing, and co-writing the film.

The Script: In his biography of Audrey Hepburn, Alexander Walker suggests that Fran Kubelik is the first woman in American movies to engage in promiscuity and retain the sympathy of the audience. Walker sees Fran as helping to make possible Hepburn's character Holly Golightly in *Breakfast At Tiffany's*. The stars have always said that only 30-some pages of the script were finished when filming started. Shirley MacLaine told interviewer James Lipton that Wilder and Diamond listened to some of her musings on the set ("Why do people have to love people, anyway?") and incorporated those observations into Fran's speeches.

The Wilder Mensch: Dr Dreyfuss is the one who treats Bud decently. He teaches Bud to "be a *Mensch*"—to be a human being, a person of integrity. When Bud quits his job by telling Sheldrake that "the old payola won't work anymore," he explains to the puzzled boss that he is simply "following doctor's orders."

Meaningful Objects: Bud's apartment key resembles the key to the executive washroom. He finally recognizes this irony when he tosses the washroom key to Sheldrake and tells him that he is "all washed up" at Consolidated Life. Initially, Bud regards his junior executive-model bowler hat as a sign of his rising status at the firm. Fittingly, he plunks it on the head of the janitor as he walks out after quitting. Fran is personalized by her carnation, which she slips into Bud's lapel when he first goes in to see Sheldrake. Her reduced self-esteem is conveyed by the broken compact mirror, which she says makes her look the way she feels. This prop is brilliantly used as a tool for revealing wordlessly to Bud the knowledge that Fran is the woman Sheldrake is taking to the apartment. Sheldrake's mercenary nature is suggested by the hundred-dollar bill he crassly peels off a wad of cash as his Christmas present for Fran. Wilder frames this shot beautifully. Sheldrake's extended hand offers the hundred while Fran rivets him with a look of complete loathing.

The Visual Element: Wilder's widescreen compositions often convey meaning wordlessly. The panoramic shots of the workers at Consolidated Life visually capture their insignificance. (Wilder's inspiration was King Vidor's *The Crowd*.) Bud is literally one person out of hundreds toiling away. His loneliness is conveyed by the shot of Bud scrunched up at night on the long park bench that recedes far into the background. On the front stoop of Bud's building, a single shot is able to include both Bud hiding in the shadows and an office executive coming down the steps referring to Bud as a "schnook." The deep-focus shots inside the apartment capitalize on the appeal of Alexander Trauner's set design. A girl from a bar calls Bud's apartment "snugsville," and this deep-space camerawork often permits us to see at once the intimacy of living room, bedroom, and kitchen.

The Verdict: A true original, the film honestly examines how easily and unintentionally we compromise ourselves and how rare it is to rise above it. The bitter-sweet tone is irresistible. *5/5*

One, Two, Three (1961)

Director: Billy Wilder
Writers: Billy Wilder & I A L Diamond, based on Ferenc Molnár's one-act play
Cast: James Cagney (MacNamara), Horst Bucholz (Otto Piffl), Pamela Tiffin (Scarlett Hazeltine), Arlene Francis (Phyllis MacNamara), Howard St John (Mr Hazeltine), Hans Lothar (Schlemmer), Lilo Pulver (Ingeborg), Karl Lieffen (Fritz), Red Buttons (MP), 115 minutes

Story: C R MacNamara is the head of Coca-Cola in West Berlin. He lives and talks at full throttle, planning to distribute Coke in Russia, barking orders at his assistant, fooling around with his secretary, and most of all, hoping for a transfer to the London office. When Mr Hazeltine from headquarters in Atlanta asks him to look after Scarlett, his seventeen-year-old daughter who will arrive in Berlin, Mac sees the perfect chance to get the London job.

Scarlett, however, turns out to be a handful. Weeks pass before Mac learns that she has been sneaking out at night to go to East Berlin. There she has met and married a defiant young Communist named Otto Piffl. Mac concocts a scheme to make Piffl look like an American spy so that he will be arrested in East Berlin. He then discovers that Scarlett is pregnant and that Mr Hazeltine and his wife will soon arrive to join her. In a blur of activity, Mac comes up with a plan to liberate Piffl from East Berlin, and in three frantic hours he further orchestrates a make-over for Piffl that turns the grubby Marxist into the tailored image of an acceptable son-in-law. He does such a good job that Hazeltine awards the London job to Piffl. Mac, fittingly, is moved to Atlanta as head of procurement.

Subtext: The film uses farce to satirize ruthlessness, whether it concerns the Coca-Cola capitalism of MacNamara, the angry Marxism of Piffl, or the teenage hedonism of Scarlett. Cagney's commanding screen presence dominates the film. MacNamara is brash, shrewd, confident, fast-thinking, fast-talking, imperious, tasteless, and completely unashamed. He exudes, good and bad, much of what Wilder finds distinctive of America. When a German newspaperman encounters this 'ugly American,' the journalist asks him, "Do you think you can bribe a member of the German press?" MacNamara ponders the new challenge. "I don't know," he replies, "I never tried." In bargaining with Russian trade officials who offer seats at the ballet for Coke distribution rights, MacNamara says, "No culture. Just cash." The words could be his personal credo.

Background: Transplanting a 1926 play into the politics of the Cold War brought out farcical comedy in a serious political subject. A month after Wilder started location shooting, the East Germans closed the border and built the beginnings of the Berlin Wall. The film crew finished their schedule in Munich. Cagney aired his grievances about the film in his auto-biography. He objected to the machine-gun pace of the dialogue, but about Wilder he made a comment that also applies to MacNamara: 'He was overly bossy, full of noise, a pain. Still, we did a good picture together.' The scene in which Cagney inspects the tailor's rack of suits required fifty-two takes. Despite some good reviews, the picture failed to earn back its costs.

The Script: Many film-makers scrupulously avoid contemporary references so as not to date their work. This script, however, revels in the world of 1961. Part of its appeal comes from the array of topical jokes: Roger Maris home runs, competing soft drinks, *Spartacus,* Sputnik missile shots, Huntley and Brinkley, TV westerns, Princess Grace, striped toothpaste, Benzedrine and bikinis.

The Wilder Mensch: As Kevin Lally points out, Phyllis MacNamara is the only non-obsessed character in the film. She represents stability and good sense, and when she asserts herself in the third act she finally succeeds in bringing out the best in her husband.

Meaningful Objects: MacNamara's umbrella reflects his hope of eventually landing the London job. His cuckoo clock, which plays 'Yankee Doodle' while a miniature Uncle Sam pops out, symbolizes his capitalist-imperialist nature. When Mac offers the clock to Piffl as a wedding present, he wraps it in a copy of the *Wall Street Journal*, knowing it will get Piffl detained by the East German authorities.

The Visual Element: It is a film of big spaces—expansive offices, airplane runways, a hotel ballroom, the wide boulevards leading to the Brandenburg Gate—and the widescreen camera utilizes all the space well. Favoring medium and long shots, Wilder designs his images so that action in foreground and background often comment on each other. In one example, as Scarlett talks to Phyllis, the MacNamaras' maid appears in the far back of the shot wearing Scarlett's mink coat, which she has received as a gift, a sign of Piffl's anti-materialistic influence on his wife.

The Verdict: The finger-snapping, heel-clicking spirit of this comedy on caffeine takes some getting used to, but those who can enter its world will be satisfied. *4/5*

Irma La Douce (1963)

Director: Billy Wilder
Writers: Billy Wilder & I A L Diamond, based on the play by Alexandre Breffort
Cast: Jack Lemmon (Nestor), Shirley MacLaine (Irma), Lou Jacobi (Moustache), Bruce Yarnell (Hippolyte), 147 minutes

Story: In the red-light district of Paris, a zealous new patrolman named Nestor Patou arrests everybody in the Hotel Casanova, including Irma la Douce (or Irma the Sweet), whom he has just met. But since his police inspector is a regular customer at the hotel, Nestor loses his job. Dejected, he later complains about life's unfairness with Moustache, the proprietor of a nearby bistro. Nestor then rescues Irma from her bullying pimp Hippolyte and accompanies Irma home for what becomes a tender night of conversation and love. Irma is thrilled with Nestor as a replacement for Hippolyte, but Nestor is tortured by the thoughts of her many customers. With the help of Moustache, Nestor disguises himself as Lord X, a visiting Englishman who only wants conversation from Irma and who pays her lavishly. Nestor must work nights to obtain this money, and Irma notices that Nestor is increasingly tired and distant. She becomes attracted to Lord X and estranged from Nestor.

Soon Nestor is plotting again with Moustache how to dispose of the Englishman. When Nestor throws the disguise into the Seine, he is arrested for murder. He escapes from prison after hearing that Irma is pregnant. Nestor stages a surprise reappearance as Lord X to clear himself and then marries Irma minutes before she gives birth to their daughter.

Subtext: According to biographer Ed Sikov, Wilder, when asked what *Irma* was about, replied, "It's a marvelous subject—it's the story of a man who is jealous of himself."

Background: Wilder and Diamond became increasingly interested in exploring the premise of the source material, and in the adaptation they removed all the songs from what had been a successful stage musical. André Prévin won an Oscar for his new film score. An uncredited Louis Jourdan reads the opening narration. James Caan appears in the walk-on part of the baseball-loving soldier.

The Script: The collaboration this time resulted in a rare misfire (although, surprisingly, the film proved to be Wilder's biggest commercial success). The culprit is a ponderous sense of pace. Ed Sikov suggests that

Wilder intentionally sought a more deliberate pacing as a contrast to the rapidity of *One, Two, Three* ('Contemplation, not speed, is Wilder's goal'), but an equally likely explanation is that after the success of *The Apartment* Wilder was simply more susceptible to directorial self-indulgence. Almost every scene continues too long. Jokes mildly funny the first time (the spraying seltzer bottle, Lord X's movie references) become belabored running gags.

The Wilder Mensch: Moustache is a worldly-wise father figure who is not quite as compelling as he should be. Wilder had originally sought Charles Laughton for the part, but his friend from *Witness For The Prosecution* was dying of cancer.

Meaningful Objects: The meat market ("the stomach of Paris") where Nestor moonlights slicing carcasses becomes a none-too-subtle metaphor for life on the Rue Casanova.

The Visual Element: The lush color and Alexander Trauner's pleasingly artificial sets work well with the widescreen cinematography. The film's exaggerated qualities suggest a live-action cartoon.

The Verdict: The characters come to life only in the charming scene when Irma first takes Nestor home with her. *2/5*

"If People Don't Go To See A Picture, Nobody Can Stop Them"

As audiences and their tastes changed, Wilder's films became less popular, but some of his later projects are among his most interesting.

Kiss Me, Stupid (1964)

Director: Billy Wilder
Writers: Billy Wilder & I A L Diamond, based on a play by Anna Bonacci
Cast: Dean Martin (Dino), Kim Novak (Polly the Pistol), Ray Walston (Orville J Spooner), Felicia Farr (Zelda), Cliff Osmond (Barney Millsap), Barbara Pepper (Big Bertha), 124 minutes

Story: Dino, the charming and lecherous Las Vegas singer, stops for gas on his way to Hollywood in Climax, Nevada. The oily filling-station attendant is Barney Millsap, a would-be lyricist who writes pop songs with Orville Spooner, the local piano teacher. By disabling Dino's car, Barney contrives a scheme to have Dino sing a Spooner and Millsap tune on an upcoming TV special. Barney directs Dino to Orville's house for the night, but when Orville sees that the oversexed Dino is already craving a bedmate, he calls off the deal. Orville's wife Zelda ran a Dino fan club in high school, and Orville will take no chances that this Rat Pack Casanova will make her another conquest.

Barney is way ahead of him. He advises Orville to start an argument with Zelda and make her leave. Barney will go to the local bar, the Belly Button, and bring back waitress/hooker Polly the Pistol to pose as Zelda. With a new 'Mrs Spooner,' Orville can safely audition songs for Dino. In the middle of this masquerade, Zelda unexpectedly returns home, peeks through the window, glimpses Orville with Polly, and heads to the Belly Button herself to drown her sorrows. Big Bertha, the proprietress, sends Zelda to Polly's empty trailer to sleep it off.

Meanwhile, Polly and Orville now have second thoughts. The domesticity of carrying out their scheme has made them both tender and reflective. Polly is charmed by her one night as a housewife; Orville realizes that he doesn't want to offer Dino even a Zelda stand-in. He angrily throws Dino out, and then Orville and the flattered and touched 'Mrs Spooner' romantically turn out the lights. Dino heads for the Belly Button in search of a woman. He is directed to Polly's trailer, where an amazed Zelda welcomes him and listens to Dino's story of dinner with the piano teacher and his wife and his painful eviction. Praising Orville's songs while she rubs Dino's sore back, Zelda also does some thinking. The next morning Dino is gone, having left Zelda $500. He later performs a Spooner and Millsap song on the TV show. A happy Orville and Zelda reconcile, each with a closely kept secret.

Subtext: Can adultery save a marriage, even under the unlikeliest circumstances? Wilder challenges the rigidity of middle-class morality and small-town life, where keeping up appearances can sap one's honesty. Before this sounds too lofty, one should also recall the generally sleazy tone. The film savors rubbing the audience's face in all the libidinous hustling.

Background: Ira Gershwin wrote new lyrics to some discarded songs he and George had tried to sell in their early years, and these became the Spooner and Millsap tunes for the movie. Peter Sellers filmed for four weeks as Orville before a near-fatal series of heart attacks necessitated a new actor. The film suffers for the change. Orville's jealousy would almost surely have seemed more comically vulnerable and naughty and less ruthless and crude with Sellers playing the part.

The film was condemned by the Catholic Legion of Decency, the first movie to receive the 'C' rating since Tennessee Williams' *Baby Doll.* United Artists decided to distribute it in limited release through its art-house subsidiary, Lopert Films. American critics excoriated the film, except for the two dissenting voices of Bosley Crowther (who said the film was 'as moral as a preacher's Sunday sermon') and Joan Didion. In what became one of his most often quoted quips, Wilder said that the overall reaction was so vitriolic that he and Diamond felt like the parents of "a two-headed child [who didn't] dare to have intercourse."

The Script: The first hour probably needs to integrate Polly into the story sooner, but the final forty minutes or so (after Zelda peeks through the window) are a beauty of plotting. Dramatic inevitability, poetic justice, logic and emotion all dovetail in an effortlessness that appears to be merely the natural outcome of these curious events. When the housewife and the hooker meet up the morning after, we hear the musings of a real (if unconventional) moralist. Polly sees a lot of married men in the line of duty, so she knows what heels they can be. She tells Zelda to hold on to the good one she has.

The Wilder Mensch: Polly and Zelda are among Wilder's most life-affirming characters (just as Barney is probably the most loathsomely self-serving). The open-heartedness and maturity of the women and the sordid calculations of Barney tug poor Orville between his love for his wife and his itch to be famous. One of the film's truths is that Dino and Barney are essentially brothers under the skin. Take away the fame, money and charm of Dino and you have Barney.

Meaningful Objects: Zelda's well-formed sewing dummy elicits Dino's dehumanizing lust and Orville's jealousy. The torso has no head, no arms, no legs—just all the parts that interest Dino. Zelda gives Polly the $500 Dino left, and Polly returns Orville's wedding ring to Zelda, a trade emphasizing that the roles we play sometimes unlock truths about our real selves.

The Visual Element: Alexander Trauner's production design is a triumph of tawdriness. Joan Didion, writing in *Vogue*, expressed what the Climax, Nevada, of Trauner and Wilder externalizes: 'A world... seen at dawn through a hangover, a world of cheap double entendre and stale smoke and drinks in which the ice has melted: a true country of despair.' She called it a 'profoundly affecting film.'

The Verdict: Always interesting even in its occasional clumsiness, the film offers a morality as bracing as smelling salts for an America groggy from its own exaggerated respectability. *4/5*

The Fortune Cookie (1966)

Director: Billy Wilder
Writers: Billy Wilder & I A L Diamond
Cast: Jack Lemmon (Harry Hinkle), Walter Matthau (Willie Gingrich), Ron Rich (Boom Boom Jackson), Judi West (Sandy), Cliff Osmond (Purkey), Noam Pitlik (Max), Marge Redmond (Charlotte), Sig Ruman (Professor Winterhalter), 126 minutes

Story: Sideline cameraman Harry Hinkle sustains a concussion at a football game when a player collides with him. Harry's brother-in-law, Willie Gingrich, an ambulance-chasing lawyer, eagerly prepares a lawsuit against the football league, the team, and the stadium. He needs Harry's cooperation, however. Willie explains to a hospitalized and reluctant Harry what symptoms he must feign in order to cash in. When Harry's ex-wife Sandy unexpectedly calls to inquire about Harry's condition, she pretends to be worried about Harry but is really excited by the lawsuit. Willie knows that lovesick Harry will now cooperate.

A team of lawyers representing the insurance company has other ideas. They hire their own doctors to examine Harry and set up two detectives for electronic surveillance. Boom Boom Jackson, the player who crashed into Harry, assists in his recovery. He and his team-mates buy Harry a wheelchair, and a guilt-ridden Boom Boom personally supervises Harry's physical therapy. Sandy arrives itching for a chunk of the cash to sponsor her singing career. She eventually replaces Boom Boom as Harry's chief caregiver. After alerting Harry to the detectives across the street, Willie eventually negotiates a settlement for $200,000, partly by creating a phony charity.

Harry, however, has grown tired of the people involved in the sleazy scheme, especially, he admits, himself. After the settlement, Purkey, one of the detectives, interrupts Willie and Sandy's celebration in Harry's apartment to collect his microphones. Purkey intentionally slurs Boom Boom, provoking Harry into jumping out of his wheelchair in anger. Now exposed as a fraud, Harry walks out on Sandy and Willie. He finds Boom Boom at the stadium, confesses his fakery, and reconciles with his friend.

Subtext: The trailer for the film identified the ideas explored: 'There are two kinds of people in the world. Those who will do anything for money, and those who will do *almost* anything.' Harry Hinkle's love for his ex-wife places him momentarily in the second group. He abandons the plan when he comes to see that Sandy belongs in the first group.

Background: A big sports fan, Wilder got the idea for the film from watching pro football on TV. According to biographer Kevin Lally, when he saw a player topple onto a spectator, Wilder said, "That's a movie, and the guy underneath is Lemmon." Walter Matthau suffered a heart attack when filming was nearly completed, and the production had to shut down until his return.

The Script: A good rather than great effort, the script has a solid structure and some wonderful lines. One of the highlights showcases Willie in the large offices of the rival attorneys, lecturing them on the case, slithering around endless shelves of law books, and citing precedents. There are lapses too, however. Harry's incessantly crying mother, Willie's obnoxious kids, and the monocled Swiss specialist are simply tiresome clichés rather than effective comic caricatures. Even Sandy is given no redeeming traits, though her venality seems to contain some self-awareness. In one poignant moment when Sandy rides with Boom Boom from the airport to Harry's apartment, Boom Boom describes the accident and his regret over running into Harry after trying to get five more yards. Sandy knows all about it. Sometimes you want those extra five yards, she says wearily, "and somebody just gets in the way." Harry is the quintessential guy who gets in the way.

The Wilder Mensch: Boom Boom is the lone person of integrity, but this character doesn't come to life very fully. The friendship between Harry and Boom Boom isn't as believable as it needs to be for the ending to work.

Meaningful Objects: The football and the game of catch Harry and Boom Boom improvise in the final scene represent the reciprocity of friendship. In the hospital room when Willie first proposes the scheme, he tells Harry he is offering him a fortune on a silver platter. Unfortunately, he gestures with the bedpan he is holding, a wonderful example of the gap between Willie's salesmanship and reality.

The Visual Element: The ample widescreen compositions recall Wilder's work in *The Apartment*. Deep spaces and minimal editing give the audience viewing options.

The Verdict: The chemistry between Lemmon and Matthau in this, their first teaming, and Matthau's star-making, Oscar-winning performance give the satire its bite. *3/5*

The Private Life Of Sherlock Holmes (1970)

Director: Billy Wilder
Writers: Billy Wilder & I A L Diamond, based upon the characters created by Sir Arthur Conan Doyle
Cast: Robert Stephens (Sherlock Holmes), Colin Blakely (Dr Watson), Genevieve Page (Gabrielle Valladon), Christopher Lee (Mycroft Holmes), Tamara Toumanova (Madame Petrova), Clive Revill (Rogozhin), Irene Handl (Mrs Hudson), Mollie Maureen (Queen Victoria), Stanley Holloway (Gravedigger), 125 minutes

Story: Fifty years after the death of Dr John Watson, the chronicler and companion of the great Sherlock Holmes, his dispatch box is opened in the vault of a London bank. It contains accounts of special cases that Watson withheld from publication. In one, a ship's captain reports a murder at sea, and Watson asks Holmes for the chance to examine the crime scene first himself. In his eagerness, however, Watson goes to the wrong cabin with unexpected comic results. In another case, Inspector Lestrade takes Holmes to a rented room with a corpse on the floor and all the furniture and objects nailed to the ceiling. Holmes correctly deduces that Watson himself contrived the bizarre puzzle to distract the great detective from his cocaine habit. In a third case, a famous Russian ballerina offers Holmes a Stradivarius if he will father a child with her. Flattered, Holmes confesses that he would only disappoint her; his five happy years with Dr Watson, he hints, suggest a different sort of sexual attraction.

The longest case concerns a beautiful mystery woman suffering from amnesia. Holmes gradually assembles some clues. The woman, a Belgian named Gabrielle Valladon, seeks her missing husband, who was working on a secret project. The strange case eventually involves Holmes' brother Mycroft, cages of canaries, middle-aged midgets, Trappist monks, a garrulous gravedigger, the Loch Ness Monster, and Queen Victoria herself. At its conclusion, Holmes is uncharacteristically humbled and saddened by his involvement with the unforgettable Gabrielle.

Subtext: The film is a heartfelt, elegiac look at friendship and the human side of the famous detective.

Background: Wilder had long intended a play or film based on Sherlock Holmes. The popularity of the epic genre, however, was waning when this film was completed at a running time of nearly three hours (longer with the intermission). The distributor, United Artists, wanted a two-hour version that would allow exhibitors more showings per day. Wilder finally compromised. The sequences on board ship and with the upside-down room were removed along with a prologue involving Watson's grandson and a flashback concerning Holmes' first crush. The producers of a 1994 laser disc version of the movie discovered some soundless video of the shipboard sequence and audio for the upside-down room scene. They also interviewed editor Ernest Walter, who discussed working with Wilder and explained the deletions from the film.

The Script: Some enterprising publisher specializing in film should look into printing the complete shooting script. It features some of Wilder and Diamond's very best work. The interplay between Holmes and Watson is always sharp. Ernest Walter said that Wilder had worked intermittently for ten years on the script, and it shows in every scene.

The Wilder Mensch: Dr Watson, as played by Colin Blakely, makes for a wonderfully loyal protecting force and voice of concern. The deleted material of the upside-down room concludes with Watson threatening to move out of Baker Street if Holmes doesn't refrain from the needle. Holmes graciously makes what he calls the simple choice between a bad habit and a good companion: "I'm often accused of being cold and unemotional, and I admit to it. And yet in my own cold, unemotional way, I'm very fond of you, Watson." It is a genuinely moving remark. The humanity of the two characters certainly emerges in the shortened version, but the lost forty minutes would have made viewers even more comfortable with Holmes and Watson as people.

Meaningful Objects: Gabrielle's parasol code advances the plot, adds mystery, and becomes the means for her farewell to Holmes. The opening title sequence ranks with the best in Wilder's career and perhaps in anyone's. As the key themes from Miklós Rózsa's beautiful music are introduced, including a plaintive violin solo, we see memorabilia that evoke the personality of Holmes removed from the dispatch box and held before the camera: the deerstalker cap, the meerschaum pipe, a syringe, a snow globe with the likeness of Victoria.

The Visual Element: The lost footage is more regrettable since famed production designer Alexander Trauner does some of his best work in this film. Cinematographer Christopher Challis gives the film a rich, period atmosphere. The location scenes in Scotland are exciting in their epic scope.

The Verdict: On the all-time wish list of Films That Should Have Never Been Tampered With, this movie ranks with *The Magnificent Ambersons*. 4/5

Avanti! (1972)

Director: Billy Wilder
Writers: Billy Wilder & I A L Diamond, based on the play by Samuel Taylor
Cast: Wendell Armbruster III (Jack Lemmon), Juliet Mills (Pamela Piggott), Clive Revill (Carlo Carlucci), Edward Andrews (J J Blodgett), 145 minutes

Story: Wendell Armbruster, a successful and driven corporate executive, has hurried to Ischia to claim the body of his father. While impatiently waiting for the morgue to open, he learns from Carlucci, the local hotel manager, that the fatal car crash that killed his father also took the life of a woman. Later in the hotel, Wendell is further shocked to hear from Pamela Piggott, the dead woman's daughter, that for a decade Wendell's strait-laced father has been spending a romantic month each year with Pamela's mother at the same hotel.

When the corpses of the departed parents suddenly disappear, Wendell assumes that Pamela has carried out her suggestion to have them buried at their beloved resort. He intends for his father a media-rich American funeral complete with Henry Kissinger and Billy Graham. Wendell cautiously asks Pamela to dinner to test his suspicions. He soon discovers, however, that the bodies are being held by a local family whose vineyards were damaged in the car crash. Wendell pays them off.

His dinner with Pamela has initiated a recreation of the romantic rituals observed by their parents. Back at the hotel in the early morning, a shocked Wendell follows Pamela as she sheds her clothes for a dawn swim in the Mediterranean, another habit of their parents. Wendell dives in to prevent such a display but then accompanies her instead. Meanwhile, a hotel valet with blackmail on his mind and photographs of Wendell and Pamela sunbathing is killed in Pamela's room by a chambermaid he has seduced and abandoned. Pamela moves into Wendell's room, and as with their parents, their affair eventually continues. Wendell agrees to bury their parents in Italy. He returns to America with the corpse of the valet to replace his father and with plans to meet Pamela in Ischia for one month each year.

Subtext: Wilder followed the anomaly of his wistful Sherlock Holmes film with another elegiac work. In *Avanti!* the life of respectability, routine,

82

and rectitude measures up pretty poorly against the relaxation and joy of one illicit month a year in Ischia. The film shows that our everyday lives can calcify into a disguise that masks us from our real selves. But, as Bernard F Dick observes, the final act maintains the film's middle-aged point of view. Wendell and Pamela, like their parents, accept compromise. They 'give society eleven months of the year' and reserve one for each other. Wilder's comments to Michel Ciment described the film as "a love story between a son and his father."

Background: Wilder tried out a few unsuccessful substitute collaborators (Julius J Epstein, Norman Krasna, Luciano Vincenzoni) until Iz Diamond, who had been working on *40 Carats*, was free to assist him on this project. Juliet Mills happily put on twenty-five pounds to play Pamela Piggott. She told Ed Sikov in 1997 that working on the film was the highlight of her life. She also described Wilder's great disappointment when the movie lost money.

The Script: The main change between Samuel Taylor's play and the film is the hardening of Wendell's character. He is a man running the rat race at full, dehumanizing speed. At dinner with Pamela, he excuses a businessman's casual affairs but condemns his father's adultery because his father actually cared for Pamela's mother. Later, as he swims out to Pamela on the rock where she suns herself, Wendell's shorts slip off. Emotional exposure follows physical exposure, and for the first time Wendell begins to acknowledge the many stresses in his life. It's the moment he begins to change.

The Wilder Mensch: Carlucci operates mostly at the level of the plot. The upshot of his frenzied activity unites Wendell and Pamela, but the primary motive seems to be problem solving and efficiency rather than matchmaking. Wilder told Clive Revill, who turns in a wonderfully likable performance as Carlucci, to think of the character as the Toscanini of the hotel. Carlucci seemingly likes the rude, imperious Wendell because he senses that buried inside Wendell Armbruster III is a man like Wendell Armbruster II. Carlucci helps to bring that man out.

Meaningful Objects: The feather Pamela places in her hat becomes a sign of her open, easy spirit, like Cyrano de Bergerac's plume. When Wendell and Pamela wear their parents' clothes for their dinner together, they find it easier to set aside their differences.

The Visual Element: The photography (by Luigi Kuveiller) captures some beautiful location scenery. The memorable scene at the morgue dramatically uses space and the single beam of sunlight. This film was the first since the late 1950s that Wilder did not shoot in widescreen. As Ed Sikov reports, the narrower aspect ratio serves better the intimate nature of the story.

The Verdict: The slower pacing takes some getting used to, and Wendell's character starts off as the executive model of the ugly American. However, the autumnal, tolerant mood of the film is deeply satisfying. *4/5*

The Front Page (1974)

Director: Billy Wilder
Writers: Billy Wilder & I A L Diamond, based on the play by Ben Hecht & Charles MacArthur
Cast: Jack Lemmon (Hildy Johnson), Walter Matthau (Walter Burns), Susan Sarandon (Peggy Grant), Carol Burnett (Mollie Malloy), Austin Pendleton (Earl Williams), David Wayne (Bensinger), Charles Durning (Murphy), Vincent Gardinia ('Honest' Pete Hartman), Harold Gould (the Mayor), Martin Gabel (Dr Eggelhoffer), Paul Benedict (Plunkett), Doro Merande (Jenny the janitress), Allen Jenkins (Telegrapher), 105 minutes

Story: In 1929 Chicago, ace reporter Hildy Johnson plans to quit his job, marry Peggy Grant, and work for her uncle in Philadelphia as an advertising man. His tyrannical editor, Walter Burns, will try anything to keep Hildy at the *Examiner*—especially on the eve of a sensational hanging. Earl Williams is scheduled to die for killing a policeman, and his execution will help re-elect a corrupt mayor and sheriff running on a law-and-order ticket.

When Williams escapes during a psychiatric examination in the sheriff's office, the press room of the Criminal Courts Building comes to life. Even Hildy springs into action at the sound of gunshots and police sirens. He delays Peggy and their trip to the train station to cover the story for Walter. Williams, wounded during his escape, literally falls into the press room from his hiding place outside the window. Hildy and Walter hide Williams in a roll-top desk until they can tear out the front page of the morning edition with the news that the *Examiner* has captured Earl Williams. Though they are eventually arrested for hiding a fugitive, Walter and Hildy expose the mayor and sheriff. An inmate in the next cell is really a state office worker rounded up in a police sweep of a brothel. This Mr Plunkett produces a signed governor's pardon for Williams. Freed from jail, Walter and Hildy race to the train station to find Peggy, but Walter still schemes to keep his best reporter.

Subtext: The Front Page develops more extensively the father/son, mentor/pupil bond between two men that first appeared in *Double Indemnity*. The comic bonding of Burns and Johnson, invigorated by their love for the newspaper game, is too strong for any woman to break. The other reporters, hearing of Hildy's engagement, joke that he is already married to Walter. These two tough-talking men display affection for each other the only way they know how—through shouts, swearing, and anger. It's the richest comic paradox of the film. The more they throw things at one another, the more tenderness they imply, perhaps a parallel to the writing partnerships of the director, which he has often compared to marriage.

Background: Producer Paul Monash enjoyed a revival of the play at the Old Vic and thought another screen version would work. Joseph L Mankiewicz was the first choice for a director. The film marks the last screen appearance for two familiar character actors, Doro Merande (who also appeared in *The Seven Year Itch* and *Kiss Me, Stupid)* and Allen Jenkins (who appeared as the garbage man in *Ball Of Fire*).

The Script: In spite of its durable theatrical history, the Hecht and MacArthur source material was changed noticeably by Wilder and Diamond. In a sense, they were merely following the precedent set by Howard Hawks, who adapted the play into the screwball romantic comedy *His Girl Friday* by making Hildy Johnson a woman. According to Hollywood lore, Hawks was reading through the play with a script girl and noticed that the dialogue played better with a man and a woman in the leads. Wilder, with his career-long interest in buddy films and male bonding, returned to the original, seeking to capitalize on the irony of a love triangle among Matthau, Lemmon, and Susan Sarandon as the odd woman out.

The replacement of the Production Code with the movie ratings system allowed Wilder and Diamond to restore the profane chatter of the press room that had been sanitized in all previous screen versions. They also sprinkled the script with some Nixonisms ("twist slowly, slowly in the wind," being a "team player") so that their story of the crusading press had a parallel to the Watergate scandal then unfolding.

The Wilder Mensch: The most stereotypical character in Hecht and MacArthur's play is Mollie Malloy, the hooker with the heart of gold. Perhaps Wilder and Diamond should have applied some of their revisions to that part since none of the screen adaptations really presents her successfully. (Mae Clark and Helen Mack had previously played Molly.) Carol Burnett's performance as Molly is the weakest in the film, though in fairness this character lacks the wit and vulnerability of the prostitute Gloria in *The Lost Weekend*.

Meaningful Objects: Walter's pocket watch becomes the basis for his last attempt to break up Hildy and Peggy. This final sequence at the train station also restores the play's classic curtain line ("That son of a bitch stole my watch!"), cut in Hawk's version due to Production Code restrictions.

The Visual Element: The crisply edited, opening montage of the typesetting and printing of a newspaper, backed by the jazzy 'Front Page Rag' by Billy May, supplies the audience with both the flavor of the era and key plot points (like the comically paradoxical headline: "COP KILLER SANE, MUST DIE").

The Verdict: It is certainly one of Wilder's least ambitious films, but the chemistry of Lemmon and Matthau, the assured ensemble work of the press room gang, and the period detail more than offset the stridency of Carol Burnett. To quote the baseball parlance the director used in an interview with *New York* magazine, the film is not a home run, but "a solid hit, perhaps driving in a few runs." *3/5*

Fedora (1978)

Director: Billy Wilder
Writers: Billy Wilder & I A L Diamond, from a novella by Thomas Tryon
Cast: William Holden (Barry Detweiler), Marthe Keller (Fedora), Hildegard Knef (Countess Sobryanski), Jose Ferrer (Dr Vando), Frances Sternhagen (Miss Balfour), Mario Adorf (Hotel desk manager), Stephen Collins (Young Barry Detweiler), Henry Fonda (Himself), Michael York (Himself), Arlene Francis (Herself), 113 minutes

Story: The world news reports the death of legendary screen star Fedora in a tragic leap before a speeding train. Veteran Hollywood producer Barry Detweiler files past the coffin reflecting on his meetings with her just weeks ago. Detweiler had been promised financial backing for his project—a screen treatment of *Anna Karenina*—but only if he could deliver the reclusive Fedora in the lead. Detweiler flew to Corfu and spied on Fedora. A strange entourage guarded her: Dr Vando, who kept her perennially youthful despite her advanced age, Miss Balfour, and the shrouded, wheelchair-bound Countess Sobryanski. After speaking with Fedora and meeting the others, Detweiler began to wonder if Fedora was being held against her will. After Fedora later came in desperation to his hotel room, he wondered if the star herself was unstable.

A week later, Detweiler heard of Fedora's death.

He has come to pay his respects. When all the mourners have left, the Countess Sobryanski confides the entourage's secret to Detweiler. The aged Countess is really Fedora, and the woman in the casket is Antonia, the Countess' illegitimate daughter. Years ago, one of Dr Vando's rejuvenation treatments went horribly wrong and disfigured Fedora. A few years into her forced retirement, Fedora heard that she had been voted an honorary Oscar. She permitted Antonia to costume herself as 'Fedora' to welcome the academy president, knowing that he would take back to

Hollywood stories of her youthful appearance. Then film offers began arriving. The masquerade continued with Antonia even submitting to an aging treatment to achieve the indeterminate age of a beauty in her prime. On one film, however, Antonia fell in love with her co-star and only then realized that becoming Fedora had robbed her of her own life. In despair Antonia attempted suicide and slid into drug addiction. Detweiler promises to keep the secret of Fedora, who has now orchestrated and presided over her own funeral and who dies shortly after.

Subtext: The film explores the cult of celebrity and its high costs, the decline of Hollywood, and most of all, the tragic struggle to cope with having outlived your epoch. As Dr Vando says, "To pump out the stomach, that is easy. The mind? That is another thing."

Background: By all accounts, the making of *Fedora* was surprisingly difficult for a director of Wilder's stature. His association with Universal gave that studio the first refusal on the project, which they exercised after reading the script. Wilder tried to peddle his screenplay to other studios. Like Joe Gillis, he found even yes-men saying no. Eventually, financial backing came from Geria Films, a German company. To make the voices of Fedora and Antonia sound more similar, Wilder had both parts dubbed by actress Inga Bunsch. The muffled soundtrack is the weakest aspect of the film.

The Script: Over the years from *Sunset Boulevard* to *Fedora*, Wilder's interest shifted from the figure of Hollywood creativity (Joe Gillis, Barry Detweiler) to the recluse. As Bernard F Dick observes in his book on Wilder, Antonia is the Joe Gillis figure in *Fedora*. Her eagerness to join the celebrity elite leads to more than she bargains for.

The most important narrative decision made by Wilder and Diamond was to reveal the secret of Fedora halfway into the film. This strategy emphasizes the emotional insights and costs of fame rather than the surprise of the plotting.

The Wilder Mensch: Barry Detweiler becomes a kind of Hollywood Greek chorus commenting on the action. His long experience in the picture business gives him a sympathetic ear and an open heart for Fedora's story. In no other Wilder film does this life-affirming figure have such a prominent place. When he leaves after the funeral, Detweiler signs the guest book with his nickname Dutch, an affectionate sign that he will keep the secrets entrusted to him.

Meaningful Objects: Detweiler lugs around his never-to-be-shot script like a relic from a bygone age. He buys 'worry beads' from the hotel manager as an anodyne for his nervous tension while he tries to contact Fedora.

Her ribboned packet of love letters (from Barrymore, Hemingway, Rach-maninoff, 'Pablo') is a fond memento of Fedora's youth. Presenting the letters to Detweiler, she calls herself "an old lady showing her medals." The electric blanket Fedora primly asks Detweiler to send her is returned to him unopened after her death. It is the final anti-climax in her tragicomic life.

The Visual Element: The elegiac tone of the movie is assisted by some striking shots: Detweiler's little launch tossed about at the dock on the rainy day that his script is rejected, Antonia being straitjacketed at night among the deserted tables at the sidewalk café.

The Verdict: At the dawn of the *Star Wars* era, this film must have seemed like a fossil. But it is full of sharp, observant lines, effective details, and haunting moments. A personality star is needed for the part(s) of Antonia/Fedora. The actresses who play the roles, competent though they are, lack the needed charisma. An uneven but consistently interesting film. *3/5*

Buddy Buddy (1981)

Director: Billy Wilder
Writers: Billy Wilder & I A L Diamond, based on the film *L'Emmerdeur*
Cast: Walter Matthau (Trabucco), Jack Lemmon (Victor Clooney), Paula Prentiss (Celia Clooney), Klaus Kinski (Dr Zuckerbrot), Joan Shawlee (Receptionist), Ed Begley Jr. (Patrolman), 96 minutes

Story: Trabucco is a hit man hired to eliminate three key witnesses in an upcoming trial. After he has dispatched the first two (with a mail bomb and a poisoned bottle of milk), he prepares for the third, a tougher assignment since police protection has increased. Trabucco checks in to a hotel across the street from the courthouse where the trial will begin at 2:00. He intends to kill the witness with a high-powered rifle from his hotel window.

In the next room, however, is Victor Clooney, a despondent television censor who intends to commit suicide because his wife has left him for a quack doctor who runs a sex clinic. Victor's comically botched attempts at suicide and teary explanations of his woes interrupt Trabucco's lethal plans. In frustration, Trabucco tells Victor that he will drive him to the sex clinic to talk to his wife. Once there, Victor is rejected again, and he returns to the hotel with nothing left to lose. Trabucco, after receiving a sedative from the sex doctor who mistook him for Victor, now finds that he cannot deliver the *coup de grâce*. Victor volunteers to fire the fatal shot. He hits one of the policemen, but on closer examination, the victim turns out to be the key witness in disguise.

Subtext: The film is a black farce, a comedy of catastrophe, recounting the calamities of Trabucco.

Background: MGM, desiring to increase its yearly output of films, wanted to remake the French comedy on which *Buddy Buddy* is based. This production marked the first time Wilder had worked at the famous studio since *Ninotchka*. Walter Matthau's son Charlie worked on the film as an associate producer. He later directed his father and Jack Lemmon in *The Grass Harp*.

The Script: A tired rather than inspired effort, the film opens with a static shot of palm trees while the opening credits roll. If the vignettes of Matthau polishing off his first two victims had been presented, for example, as a pre-credit sequence, the main titles could then have created some suspense by making the audience wonder about the reason for the murders. The satire of television censors falls flat. Though the mistaken identity of the doctor taking Trabucco for Victor produces some cleverness, the film lacks the verbal and structural wit so distinctive of Wilder.

The Wilder Mensch: Victor thinks Trabucco is a real buddy who wants to save him from suicide. This is, of course, part of the film's black humor—that the only one who seemingly cares enough to stop Victor from hurting himself only wants sufficient peace and quiet to get off a kill shot. A rarity in Wilder, there really is no life-affirming force or voice of conscience.

Meaningful Objects: The best example of the film's brush with tastelessness: Victor's wife gives her wedding ring to her doctor-lover, who melts it down to a charm that he wears around his neck—in the shape of an erect penis.

The Visual Element: The back-projection shots and the relatively simple sets give the film something of a TV-movie look.

The Verdict: Matthau's deadpan performance is effective, but it does not redeem the film. *1/5*

"Don't Bore People"

Billy Wilder is telling a story. It is 1997 and he is receiving another award, this one a life-achievement honor from the Producers Guild of America. His acceptance speech is a simple one: "An elderly man went to his doctor. The doctor said, 'What is the problem?' The man said, 'Doctor, I cannot pee.' The doctor said, 'How old are you?' The man said, 'I'm ninety.' The doctor said, 'You've peed enough.'" Wilder sits down as the audience's laughter and applause continue. The scene appears at the end of the public television documentary *Billy Wilder: The Human Comedy,* broadcast on the *American Masters* series.

Since *Buddy Buddy*, there have been no more Wilder films. His close friend and collaborator Iz Diamond died in 1988. Wilder, however, still goes in to his office as much as he can. He and his wife Audrey have now been married over fifty years. Wilder made news in 1989 when he auctioned at Christie's in New York 94 works (including a Picasso) from his famous collection of art masterpieces. The auction earned him $32.6 million. Mostly, the recent decades have brought Wilder a steady series of honors. In 1982, he was the subject of a film tribute at Lincoln Center. He received the Life Achievement Award of the American Film Institute in 1986 and similar lifetime honors from the Directors Guild of America (1985), the European Film Awards (1992), the Writers Guild (1995), and the German Film Awards (1997). He also received an Academy Fellowship in 1996 from the British Academy Awards.

His longtime writing partner I A L Diamond quoted Voltaire ('The good is the enemy of the great') in honoring Wilder at the AFI tribute. Diamond explained that often when they were working on a scene and had something that both of them thought was good, Wilder would insist that they try to make it better. Years later, Wilder made a similar point as he rejected easy explanations about his films in his conversations with Cameron Crowe. The films, he maintained, were not so much about the fun of disguise or any one thing. These devices were employed so that the movies would not bore people. It comes down to a question of what works.

Reference Materials

Books On Wilder

A few titles that were unavailable (Bernard F Dick, Maurice Zolotow) have recently been reprinted. For others currently out of print (Leland A Poague, Steve Seidman), see websites selling previously owned books like http://www.bookfinder.com and http://www.alibris.com

Billy Wilder by Axel Madsen, Indiana, US, 1969. Many photographs and quotes combine with a summary of Wilder's career and Madsen's observations on the set of *Irma La Douce*.

Billy Wilder by Bernard F Dick, Da Capo, US, 1996. An updating of his 1980 study, Dick's book takes a comparative approach to Wilder's films, grouping them into categories like 'Human Comedies,' 'Dirty Fairy Tales,' 'September Songs.' It is stimulating and engagingly written.

Billy Wilder, American Film Realist by Richard Armstrong, McFarland, UK, 2000. Armstrong perceptively discusses sixteen Wilder films, partly as reflections of American culture and society.

Billy Wilder In Hollywood by Maurice Zolotow, Limelight, US, 1977, 1992. Probably the most controversial Wilder book because of its rigid thesis about an early disappointment in love shaping Wilder's creative vision, this biography is nevertheless informative on many other points, especially Wilder's relationship with Charles Brackett.

Conversations With Wilder by Cameron Crowe, Knopf, US, 1999. This would receive my vote for the best book on Billy Wilder. It is informative, entertaining, and packed with photos. The Q&A format is reminiscent of Truffaut's book on Hitchcock. Crowe's background as a journalist (e.g. *Almost Famous*) gives him the persistence and patience to coax out explanations and reject hasty answers (albeit politely).

Double Indemnity by Richard Schickel, BFI Publishing, UK, 1992. One of the BFI Film Classics series, this enjoyable analysis is particularly good at exploring the improvements the film makes on the original novel.

Double Indemnity by Billy Wilder, California, US, 2000. One in a series of Wilder scripts currently being reprinted in facsimile editions with new introductions by Jeffrey Meyers. The other titles in the series so far are *The Lost Weekend, Stalag 17* and *Sunset Boulevard*.

The Film Career Of Billy Wilder by Steve Seidman, Redgrave, US, 1977. Seidman annotates 183 articles and books on Wilder from 1944 to 1977. A separate section lists contemporary reviews of Wilder's films. Only very recently out of print, it is extremely useful.

The Hollywood Professionals, Volume 7: Billy Wilder, Leo McCarey, by Leland A Poague, Tantivy, UK, 1980. This would receive my vote for the best little-known book on Billy Wilder. Poague's discussion of Wilder runs to 168 pages of consistently sharp, observant writing. He is especially good on the relation of Wilder's films to Lubitsch's.

On Sunset Boulevard: The Life And Times Of Billy Wilder by Ed Sikov, Hyperion, US 1998.

Wilder Times: The Life Of Billy Wilder by Kevin Lally, Henry Holt, US, 1996.

The two big, recent biographies are both superb. Lally interviewed Wilder while Sikov did not, but Sikov's book includes more extensive analysis of the films. Both books are written with wit and insight.

Wilder On Video

An alphabetical list of British Wilder videos currently available or recently deleted in the VHS/PAL format.

The Apartment (1960) 160669

Avanti! (1972) S053093—deleted

Buddy Buddy (1981) B050142—deleted

Fedora (1978) TVS9009792—deleted

The Fortune Cookie (1966) 16171S

Kiss Me, Stupid (1964) S099576—deleted

One, Two, Three (1961) S099682—deleted

The Private Life Of Sherlock Holmes (1970) S099361—not available

Sabrina Fair (1954) VHR4458

The Seven Year Itch (1955) 1043S

Some Like It Hot (1959) 16221S

The Spirit Of St Louis (1957) S011048—deleted

Stalag 17 (1953) BRP2604

Sunset Boulevard (1950) VHR4295

Witness For The Prosecution (1957) 16236S

An alphabetical list of American Wilder videos currently available in VHS, DVD, or laserdisc.

The AFI Life Achievement Awards: Billy Wilder (1986) VHS & laserdisc

The Apartment (1960) VHS (widescreen)

Avanti! (1972) VHS

Buddy Buddy (1981) VHS

Double Indemnity (1944) VHS and DVD

The Emperor Waltz (1948) VHS

Fedora (1978) laserdisc (widescreen)

A Foreign Affair (1948) VHS

The Fortune Cookie (1966) VHS (widescreen)

The Front Page (1974) VHS and DVD

Irma La Douce (1963) VHS (widescreen)

Kiss Me, Stupid (1964) VHS

The Lost Weekend (1945) VHS

Love In The Afternoon (1957) VHS

The Major And The Minor (1942) VHS

Mauvaise Graine (1933) VHS (Dubbed)

One, Two, Three (1961) VHS

The Private Life Of Sherlock Holmes (1970) VHS (an out-of-print laserdisc features some lost footage and the shooting script)

Sabrina (1954) VHS

The Seven Year Itch (1955) VHS

Some Like It Hot (1959) VHS (an out-of-print laserdisc features audio commentary by film historian Howard Suber)

The Spirit Of St Louis (1957) VHS (widescreen)

Stalag 17 (1953) VHS and DVD

Sunset Boulevard (1950) VHS

Witness For The Prosecution (1957) VHS

Wilder On The Web

http://www.reelclassics.com/Directors/Wilder/wilder.htm - Movie posters and over thirty links to pages discussing individual films.

http://www.wga.org/WrittenBy/1995/1195/wilder.htm - The transcript of an interview with Wilder on the occasion of his 1995 Career Achievement Award from the Writers Guild Foundation. Concerning screenwriting, he mentions, among other things, "that one element X that cannot be taught."

The Essential Library

Why not try other titles in the Pocket Essentials library? Each is £2.99 unless otherwise stated. Look out for new titles every month.

New: **Ridley Scott** by Brian J Robb (£3.99)
Billy Wilder by Glenn Hopp (£3.99)

Film: **Woody Allen** by Martin Fitzgerald
Jane Campion by Ellen Cheshire
Jackie Chan by Michelle Le Blanc & Colin Odell
Joel & Ethan Coen by John Ashbrook & Ellen Cheshire
David Cronenberg by John Costello (£3.99)
Film Noir by Paul Duncan
Terry Gilliam by John Ashbrook
Heroic Bloodshed edited by Martin Fitzgerald
Alfred Hitchcock by Paul Duncan
Krzysztof Kieslowski by Monika Maurer
Stanley Kubrick by Paul Duncan
David Lynch by Michelle Le Blanc & Colin Odell
Steve McQueen by Richard Luck
Marilyn Monroe by Paul Donnelley (£3.99)
The Oscars® by John Atkinson (£3.99)
Brian De Palma by John Ashbrook
Sam Peckinpah by Richard Luck
Slasher Movies by Mark Whitehead (£3.99)
Vampire Films by Michelle Le Blanc & Colin Odell
Orson Welles by Martin Fitzgerald

TV: **Doctor Who** by Mark Campbell (£3.99)

Books: **Cyberpunk** by Andrew M Butler (£3.99)
Philip K Dick by Andrew M Butler (£3.99)
Noir Fiction by Paul Duncan

Culture:**Conspiracy Theories** by Robin Ramsay (£3.99)

Available at all good bookstores, or send a cheque to: **Pocket Essentials (Dept BW), 18 Coleswood Rd, Harpenden, Herts, AL5 1EQ, UK**. Please make cheques payable to 'Oldcastle Books.' Add 50p postage & packing for each book in the UK and £1 elsewhere.

US customers can send $5.95 plus $1.95 postage & packing for each book to: **Trafalgar Square Publishing, PO Box 257, Howe Hill Road, North Pomfret, Vermont 05053, USA**. tel: 802-457-1911, fax: 802-457-1913, e-mail: tsquare@sover.net

Customers worldwide can order online at **www.pocketessentials.com**, **www.amazon.com** and at all good online bookstores.